PHILISTINES

MAXIM GORKY

PHILISTINES

ENGLISH VERSION BY

DUSTY HUGHES

AMBER LANE PRESS

All rights whatsoever in this English stage version of
Philistines are strictly reserved and application for performance, etc. should be made before rehearsal to:

Margaret Ramsay Ltd.
14a Goodwin's Court
St Martin's Lane
London WC2N 4LL

No performance may be given unless a licence has been
obtained.

First published in 1986 by
Amber Lane Press Ltd.
9 Middle Way
Oxford OX2 7LH

Printed in Great Britain by
Cotswold Press Ltd., Oxford

Copyright © Dusty Hughes, 1985

ISBN 0 906399 65 3

BACKGROUND TO THE PLAY

In 1898 Maxim Gorky wrote a clumsy, breathless letter to Chekhov in the secret hope that it would begin a literary friendship. He had decided to make Chekhov his mentor, and when he received a warm response Gorky initiated a lengthy correspondence that touched on every aspect of writing. Within a year, Russia's most famous literary primitive, and patron saint of the down-and-outs, was given a gold watch inscribed 'To Gorky from Chekhov'.

Gorky was used to being patronised, but his relationship with Chekhov was a closer one than he had ever experienced with another writer. The condescension he had frequently to swallow was the reason he still clung to his home town of Nizhni Novgorod (now re-named Gorky) and why he refused the attempts of various literary entrepreneurs to introduce him to the Moscow *beau monde*.

But his days as a provincial were numbered. In Nizhni his activities included organising yuletide sleigh rides for destitute children and fighting a battle to get a wonderfully talented local tavern singer into the snobbish town choir. During this period even his philanthropic work could have got him into trouble for 'unauthorised community fund activities' but he had already gone much further. By 1900 he had acquired a duplicating machine and had begun to write and distribute 'proclamations to the workers' whenever there was a strike or a local dispute. His police file was beginning to bulge with black marks.

By 1901, however, Gorky had moved to Moscow where he became a celebrity (known as 'the barefooted tramp') with the fame of a pop-star. In the summer of that year he rented a house in Yalta, a few hundred yards from where Chekhov was living, and he had his first taste of the glamour of theatrical life when the actors of the Moscow Art Theatre came down for their traditional summer break.

Chekhov persuaded Gorky to write a play and introduced him to Stanislavsky and Nemirovich-Danchenko, who were planning to move the Art Theatre into an exciting new building. Though the Art Theatre company were not all radicals, there was still a shared feeling that Russia was on the verge of a great change. As Gorky often felt a greater affinity with theatre people than with the *literati* (who cast him in the role of bumpkin) he needed little encouragement to write for the stage. He began work immediately on two plays: *Philistines* and *The Lower Depths*.

By the end of the year, however, Gorky had attracted far too much attention to himself. On a trip to St Petersburg he went to a rally to celebrate the liberation of the peasants and was noticed in a restaurant 'behaving in a revolutionary manner'. He was eventually arrested in his home town after being found in possession of his incriminating duplicator and sent to prison. *Philistines* was finished and the Art Theatre courageously decided to go ahead with the play as their first production in the new theatre.

Stanislavsky did his best to get Gorky released from jail but it was Tolstoy (who had met Gorky a year before) who secured his reprieve by appealing to the Tsar's brother-in-law. Gorky's ill-health (he had had tuberculosis) was used as a pretext to commute the sentence to exile in the Crimea.

When *Philistines* was offered to the censor in 1902 it was refused a licence. But the Art Theatre persisted, and finally the play was cleared for 'members only' performances. Certain key lines had to be cut from the text as they were considered too progressive by the authorities, for example, "The man who works is the master here too."

On the opening night the box-office staff and the usherettes were all agents of the secret police, checking to see if any non-members of the theatre (obviously a more corruptible group) were trying to sneak in.

The Art Theatre clearly couldn't continue to give only 'exclusive' performances of *Philistines* so they decided to take the play on tour. In every town they had to obtain clearance from the censor. In Bialystock it provoked a riot, with civil guards, the police and demonstrators all fighting in the streets; there was one fatality.

Though *Philistines* has been presented in a number of versions in America the play has been neglected in Britain where it has never, until now, had a major professional production.

The text given here is the complete one. There are many small areas of repetition that can justifiably be cut. Certainly the RSC production benefited enormously from judicious pruning and the play was in consequence much lighter on its feet.

Dusty Hughes, 1985

CHARACTERS

VASILY VASILYEVICH BESSEMENOV: 58, a prosperous house-painter, head of his guild

AKULINA IVANOVNA : 52, his wife

PYOTR : their son, 26, a student expelled from university

TATYANA : their daughter, 27, a schoolmistress

NIL : 27, their foster-son, a train-driver

PERCHIKHIN : 50, a distant relative, a bird-catcher

POLYA : 21, his daughter, a seamstress who works during the day for the BESSEMENOVS

YELENA KRIVTSOVA : 24, a jail-warden's widow who lodges with the family

TETEREV (Terenty Khrisanfovich): choirsinger and lodger

SHISHKIN : a lodger

TSVETAEVA (Masha): 25, a schoolmistress and a friend of TATYANA'S

STEPANIDA : the cook

AN OLD WOMAN

THE DOCTOR

A YOUNG BOY : house-painter's apprentice

The play takes place in a small provincial town. (*NB:* for this R.S.C. production details of The Moscow Art Theatre set have been omitted to avoid confusion.)

This new English version of *Philistines* was first presented by the Royal Shakespeare Company at The Other Place, Stratford-upon-Avon, on 30 March 1985. It was directed by John Caird with the following cast:

TATYANA	Fiona Shaw
POLYA	Lesley Manville
PYOTR	Sean Baker
BESSEMENOV	David Burke
AKULINA	Margery Mason
STEPANIDA	Ruby Head
PERCHIKHIN	Mark Dignam
TETEREV	Clive Russell
NIL	Tom Mannion
YELENA	Anna Calder-Marshall
SHISHKIN	Christopher Wright
TSVETAEVA	Mary Jo Randle
A YOUNG BOY	Paul Basson
PEASANTS	Mary Jo Randle
	Christopher Wright
DOCTOR	Griffith Jones

Piano: John Woolf
Literal translation by Helen Rappaport

ACT ONE

Five in the evening. An autumn dusk. The room is almost dark.

TATYANA, *propped up on one elbow on the couch, is reading aloud.* POLYA *is sitting at the table, sewing.*

TATYANA: "Then the moon rose. How strange, it was such a sad little moon, but it cast so much soft silvery-blue light over the earth . . . " [*She drops the book.*]Well, it's dark enough in here.

POLYA: I'll light a lamp.

TATYANA: No, don't bother. I don't want to read any more.

POLYA: He puts it so beautifully, doesn't he? It's so sad, it does something to me in here. [*Pause.*] I can't wait to find out how it all ends. Are they going to get married?

TATYANA: [*tetchily*] That's hardly the point.

POLYA: He's not my type. Could you love someone like that?

TATYANA: I don't see why not.

POLYA: I do. He's boring, isn't he? The constant complaining. Not being able to make up his mind one way or the other. I like a man who knows what he wants.

TATYANA: [*quietly*] Like Nil. Does Nil know what he wants?

POLYA: Oh, yes. Nil knows what he wants.

TATYANA: What exactly does he want?

POLYA: He can explain it much better than I can. He wants to expose all the evil that's in rich, greedy people . . . because he hates them so much.

TATYANA: How can you tell who is evil and who isn't?

POLYA: Ask Nil. He knows.

> [POLYA *takes the book out of* TATYANA's *lap.* TATYANA *doesn't look at her.*]

It's beautifully written. When a woman is described so sympathetically; good-natured, simple, straightforward, it makes you feel a better person yourself.

TATYANA: Your naiveté does make me smile sometimes. To be honest with you, the whole saga gets on my nerves. I've never heard of a woman like that. Or of such a country estate. Not to mention the river and the moon! It's just an invention. Books never show us

things as they are. They don't tell us what it's like to
be you and me.

POLYA: That's because we're not interesting enough to be in
a novel.

TATYANA: [*irritated, ignores her*] People who write books don't
like people like me. It's either heaven or hell for
them, nothing in between. Nothing in the middle
where ordinary people are trapped.

POLYA: Whenever I think of a writer I think of someone who
is wise and kind. I'd move mountains to meet a
writer!

TATYANA: [*to herself*] They never write about the things I see
around me, all the annoying and hurtful things, no,
they puff the whole thing up into a grand tragedy.
And all the nice moments are pure invention. Love
scenes are never how they are in books. Life is not
tragic. It just goes on and on without ever changing,
like a great, dark river. And your eyes get tired from
watching it and your mind gets so dulled that you
completely forget why the river flows in the first
place.

POLYA: [*thoughtfully, staring straight ahead*] All the same, I wish I
could get a look at him. I was wondering what he was
like when you were reading. Young? Old? Dark?

TATYANA: Who?

POLYA: The writer.

TATYANA: Dead.

POLYA: What a shame! How long ago? Did he die young?

TATYANA: In middle age. He drank.

POLYA: Poor creature. Why do the clever ones drink? Your
lodger, the one who sings in the choir, he's intelli-
gent and he drinks. Why is that?

TATYANA: Because he's bored and tired and fed up with everything.

[PYOTR *comes out of his room, looking as if he's
emerged from a deep sleep.*]

PYOTR: Lord, it's dark! Who's that over there?

POLYA: It's only me. And Tatyana Vasilyevna.

PYOTR: Why don't you light some lamps?

POLYA: Because we're enjoying the twilight.

PYOTR: My room smells of cheap lamp oil. It seeps out of the
old man's and into mine. When I was asleep I

dreamed I was swimming in this oily river and it was difficult to make any progress, like swimming through tar, and you couldn't see the shore or what direction you were going in. Whenever anything floated past I grabbed hold of it but it always crumbled into dust because it was rotting. Doesn't make sense. [*whistling and walking across the room*] Is it time for some tea?

POLYA: [*lighting the lamp*] I'll see to it.

[*She exits.*]

PYOTR: It's always so claustrophobic and gloomy here in the evenings. All these dreadful old things seem to swell up and get gross and heavy and start to crowd us out until there's no air left. [*bangs the sideboard with his fist*] This monument has not moved for eighteen years. Eighteen years! Life's rich tapestry goes on but the sideboard hasn't moved an inch. I was always banging my head on it when I was a kid and I still am in a way. Stupid piece of old lumber!

TATYANA: Really, you're so ridiculous. You're not doing yourself any good the way you're living at the moment.

PYOTR: Why is that?

TATYANA: You never go anywhere. Except upstairs to see Lena every evening. And that only upsets mother and father.

[*POYTR doesn't answer. He carries on whistling and pacing up and down.*]

I get so tired at the moment. All the noise at school just exhausts me. At least everything's in its right place here, and it's peaceful. Though less so since Lena's been living here. I am just worn out. It's such a long time to go until the holidays ... November ... and December ...

[*It strikes six.*]

BESSEMENOV: [*putting his head round the door of his room*] There's always an endless gabbling coming from here. Have you managed to write that petition yet?

PYOTR: Yes I have. I have managed to, thank you.

BESSEMENOV: I bet it nearly killed you.

[*He disappears, laughing.*]

TATYANA: What petition?

PYOTR: Sizov hasn't paid us for painting the roof of his barn.
         So we're suing him, that's all.

> [AKULINA *comes in with a lamp. She goes to the side-*
> *board, takes out the tea-things and starts laying the*
> *table.*]

AKULINA: Raining again. The stove's lit but it's still cold in
         here. It's an old, draughty house. Ay ay ay! I'm sorry
         to say your father's not in the best of moods. Back-
         ache, growing old. Nothing but worries and trouble
         and paying out money the whole time.

TATYANA: [*to her brother*] Were you at Yelena's last night?

PYOTR: Yes . . .

TATYANA: So. Did you have a good time?

PYOTR: Oh, you know . . . same as usual. We drank tea, sang
         a few songs, argued a bit.

TATYANA: Who with?

PYOTR: Nil and Shishkin. And me.

TATYANA: The usual argument.

PYOTR: Oh yes, it never changes. Nil went into ecstasy about
         the beauty of life . . . God, he gets on my
         nerves . . . the great prophet of the new dawn. It's
         such a joke. This golden new life of his is no more
         real than if our Rich American Uncle arrived and
         started showering us with money. And Shishkin
         decided to pontificate to me about the health-giving
         qualities of milk and the dangers of smoking. He
         even had the nerve to tell me my outlook on life was
         bourgeois!

TATYANA: It's always like that.

PYOTR: I know.

TATYANA: And Yelena. You like her?

PYOTR: Oh, she's not too bad. She's quite friendly, anyway,
         and . . . reasonably lively.

AKULINA: If you want my opinion she's a flirt. A complete
         waste of time. She seems to have company every
         evening. They all sing and dance and take tea and
         eat sweets as if there's no tomorrow. Meanwhile the
         boards of the house are rotting because madam
         hasn't saved enough money to buy a wash-stand, so
         she washes in a bowl and slops it all over the floor.

TATYANA: Do you know what happened at the social last night?
         Somov, from the town council was there. He's a

governor of my school but it was an effort for him to
even acknowledge me. I couldn't believe it but it
happened! And when judge Romanov's *mistress* came
in, he rushed across to her and bowed and kissed her
hand and practically prostrated himself. Anybody
would have thought it was the governor's wife.

AKULINA: He's completely shameless. He couldn't take the
arm of a decent girl and walk her across the room.

TATYANA: [*to her brother*] Imagine, for people like that, a schoolteacher deserves less respect than some cheap,
painted woman!

PYOTR: It's beneath you to worry about behaviour like that.
Forget all about it. In any case, the woman may be
immoral but she doesn't paint her face.

AKULINA: And how, may I ask, do you know? Have you been
nuzzling up to her recently? Your sister's been
insulted and there you are trying to stand up for the
bitch who's the cause of it all.

PYOTR: That's enough, mother.

TATYANA: It's useless trying to talk in front of mother.
[*Heavy steps are heard off-stage.*]

AKULINA: Now then, you don't need to bite my head off. And
instead of pacing up and down like that, Pyotr, why
don't you carry in the samovar? You know it's too
heavy for Stepanida, she's always complaining
about it.
[STEPANIDA *comes in with the samovar, puts it on the
floor by the table and straightens up, gasping for
breath.*]

STEPANIDA: [*to* AKULINA] This is the last time I'm going to drag
this thing around. You can take it or leave it. I
haven't got the strength in my legs any more.

AKULINA: You think we should hire a servant just to carry in
the samovar, do you?

STEPANIDA: I don't mind what you do. Get the choirboy to do it.
Wouldn't do him any harm. Pyotr Vasilyevich,
would you just lift it onto the table for me? I can't do
it, I really can't.

PYOTR: Here we go then.
[*He grunts.*]

STEPANIDA: Much obliged to you.
[*She exits.*]

AKULINA: It's an idea. Would you have a word with the choir-singer, Petya, and ask him if he'd mind carrying the samovar in future? Really!

TATYANA: [*an agonised sigh*] Oh my God, *mother!*

PYOTR: Do you want me to ask him to scrub the floors and clean the chimneys and fetch water while he's doing it?

AKULINA: [*with a disgruntled wave of the hand*] Don't be so silly. All those things get done in their own good time without his help. The samovar's a different matter.

PYOTR: Every evening, mother, you always bring up the earth-shattering question of who should bring up the samovar. Why don't you hire an odd-job-man? Nothing will happen until you do, believe me.

AKULINA: What do we need an odd-job-man for? Your father looks after all that.

PYOTR: That's only because he's so mean. I can't see the point of penny-pinching when you've got so much in the bank.

AKULINA: Shh! Be quiet! Your father will give you money in the bank if he hears you talking like that. I haven't noticed *you* putting any money in the bank.

PYOTR: Why don't you listen to me, mother!

TATYANA: [*jumping up*] Pyotr, don't! I can't stand any more of this.

PYOTR: [*going up to her*] All right, all right. I get involved in these petty squabbles without realising it.

AKULINA: Oh, that's charming! Is it forbidden to talk to your mother these days?

PYOTR: It's always the same! Every day, I feel as if my spirits have been chewed away and all I've got inside is a fine layer of ashes. Or is it rust?

AKULINA: [*calling*] Father! Come and have your tea!

PYOTR: When my period of suspension's up and I can go back to the university I shall only come back here for a week at a time and no more. I'll go to Moscow instead. I completely forgot what living at home was like in those three years away. I forgot all about meanness and petty obsessions. Living alone and not under your parents' roof is the most wonderful thing in the world.

TATYANA: What about me? Where can I go?

PYOTR: I keep telling you — go away and study.

TATYANA: Why should I? I don't want to study, I want to live. To live! Doesn't anybody in this house understand?
[AKULINA *burns her hand as she takes the teapot off the samovar.*]

AKULINA: Ouch! Hell and damnation!

TATYANA: [*to her brother*] I've no idea what it means to live. I can't imagine what it would be like. How, one wonders, does one go about it?

PYOTR: [*thoughtfully*] One must live life to the limit but . . . one must also take care.
[BESSEMENOV *enters from his room, inspects his children and sits down at the table.*]

BESSEMENOV: Have you called the lodgers?

AKULINA: [*to* PYOTR] Call them.

BESSEMENOV: Lump sugar! Why have you bought lump sugar? The number of times I've told you!

TATYANA: What difference does it make, father?

BESSEMENOV: I wasn't talking to you. I was talking to your mother. It doesn't make any difference to you, I know.

AKULINA: I bought a pound, that's all. There's a whole head of the other, but we haven't had time to break it up. Don't be angry.

BESSEMENOV: I'm not angry! All I'm saying is that lump sugar doesn't make economic sense; it's heavy and it isn't sweet enough. Buy your head and do the breaking up yourself. It makes sense to use the left-over crumbs for cooking, because they have the advantage of being light and sweeter as well. [*to* TATYANA] Why are you sighing and making faces?

TATYANA: Oh, nothing. It was nothing.

BESSEMENOV: If it was nothing, then why are you making such a fuss? Is it excruciating for you to have to listen to your father talking? I don't do it for my own benefit. It's only for you, you know. We've had our life. You've got yours ahead of you, though I've no idea how you think you're going to manage. Have you got any ambitions, either of you? You're snooty enough about the life your mother and I lead but have you got any original ideas of your own? Because that is the point really, isn't it?

TATYANA: Oh father! Do you know how many times you've said that to me?

BESSEMENOV: And no doubt I'll say it over and over again until they put me in a box. I never have a moment's peace. And we all know why that is. I must have been deranged when I had the idea of giving you both a decent education. He's been kicked out of university and you're an old maid.

TATYANA: I work . . . I . . .

BESSEMENOV: Yes, I've heard that. But what exactly is the point of it all? Nobody needs the twenty-five roubles you earn, least of all yourself. Get yourself married and settled into a respectable routine and I'll give you fifty a month.

AKULINA: [*who has been fidgeting on her chair and trying to interrupt*] Would you like a little cheese-cake, father? It's left over from dinner . . . would you like some?

[BESSEMENOV *turns on her angrily, then softens.*]

BESSEMENOV: All right, all right. Let's have the famous cheese-cake. See how your mother protects you. Like a mother goose keeping the dogs off her goslings. She's terrified in case I might say something that hurts your sensitive feelings.

[PERCHIKHIN *appears in the doorway and* POLYA *stands silently behind.*]

Aha! Look who's turned up again like a bad penny! It's the intrepid bird-man!

PERCHIKHIN: Peace be with you! To all your household! Respected grey-haired master! Handsome wife! Worthy offspring! Peace! Peace!

BESSEMENOV: Been hitting the bottle again.

PERCHIKHIN: I have been drowning my sorrows.

BESSEMENOV: Oh yes, what sorrows are these?

PERCHIKHIN: [*bows to everyone individually*] Today I sold a most precious bird, a goldfinch. This bird was precious for the most extraordinary reason. It could yodel. It could do what we call the Tyrolean warble. I had the creature for three years and I sold it. It was a terrible thing to do. I'm heartbroken. That little bird, I knew it so well. I loved that little bird.

[POLYA *smiles and gestures to her father.*]

BESSEMENOV: I can't understand why you got rid of it if you loved it so much.

PERCHIKHIN: [*holding onto the backs of the chairs as he moves around the table*] I did moderately well out of the eventual . . . transaction.

AKULINA: I don't know why you bother. You only waste your money.

PERCHIKHIN: Ah, yes. It's true. It just slips through my fingers. Can't seem to hold onto the stuff.

BESSEMENOV: Just what I said, you didn't have to sell it at all.

PERCHIKHIN: Well, yes, I did, you see. The poor creature was dying. It was going blind.

BESSEMENOV: He's not as daft as he looks!

PERCHIKHIN: It's not because I'm cunning, no, it's because I'm a horrible person, I'm utterly vile!

[PYOTR *and* TETEREV *come in.*]

TATYANA: Where's Nil?

PYOTR: He's gone off with Shishkin to a rehearsal.

BESSEMENOV: Where are they doing this play?

PYOTR: In the riding school. For the soldiers.

PERCHIKHIN: My respects to the piper of God! How would you like to come and catch tomtits with me, eh?

TETEREV: Good idea. When shall it be?

PERCHIKHIN: What about tomorrow?

TETEREV: No, not tomorrow, I'm singing at a funeral.

PERCHIKHIN: Then we should go before Mass.

TETEREV: Absolutely. Call for me. Akulina Ivanovna — was there by any chance anything left over from dinner? A bit of kasha or something like that?

AKULINA: Yes, there was, my dear. Polya, go and fetch it.

[POLYA *exits.*]

TETEREV: You're very kind. A funeral *and* a wedding today and no time for any dinner!

AKULINA: I know, I know . . .

[PYOTR *takes a glass of tea and goes through the archway into the little room, accompanied by the penetrating stare of his father and a hostile look from* TETEREV. *For a few seconds they all eat and drink in silence.*]

BESSEMENOV: You must be making a fortune this month, Terenty Khrisanfovich. People have been dropping dead like flies.

TETEREV: It hasn't been bad. A lucky streak, you might say.

BESSEMENOV: Plenty of weddings too.

TETEREV: Yes, they're wedding as if there's no tomorrow.

BESSEMENOV: If you save up all the money you've been earning this month, you can get married too.

TETEREV: Oh no, not me.

              [TATYANA *goes over to* PYOTR *and they talk quietly together.*]

PERCHIKHIN: No, don't get married. It isn't for cranks like you and me. Catching bullfinches is a much better pastime.

TETEREV: I agree.

PERCHIKHIN: The great sport of catching bullfinches! There isn't a thing that can touch it! Imagine it, the first snow has just fallen. The good earth is wearing its new white vestments like the priest at Easter. Everything is pure and shining and everywhere there's a delicate stillness. If the sun graces us with his presence as well, why then the heart simply leaps for joy! Snow is everywhere, a sprinkling of pure silver on the branches of the trees and the gold of the autumn leaves . . . and in the middle of all this incredible beauty — Whirr! Whirr! Whirr! Whirr! Suddenly a flock of red birds drops down out of the clear sky and bursts into colour on the trees like a whole field of poppies. Chirrup! Chirrup! Chirrup! Gorgeous plump little birds, strutting up and down like field-marshals — a joy to the soul! It makes me want to turn into a bullfinch on the spot just so I can roll around in the snow with them.

BESSEMENOV: A stupid bird. The bullfinch.

PERCHIKHIN: I'm a stupid old bird too.

TETEREV: Beautifully described. Just like a picture.

AKULINA: [*to* PERCHIKHIN] Look at you, you're just a great big baby.

PERCHIKHIN: I love catching birds. Is there anything on earth more beautiful than a singing bird?

BESSEMENOV: I bet you didn't know it was a sin. Catching birds.

PERCHIKHIN: I know, I know. But what can I do? I love them. It's the only thing I know how to do. And you know I always think . . . any job that's done with love has God's blessing.

BESSEMENOV: *Any* job?

PERCHIKHIN: Oh yes, any.

BESSEMENOV: And what if your job happens to be pocketing other people's worldly wealth?

PERCHIKHIN: That's not a job. That's stealing.

BESSEMENOV: Hmm. Maybe.

AKULINA: [*yawning*] Oh dear! This is all very trying. I wish time didn't drag so much in the evenings. Terenty Khrisanfovich, why don't you play us something on your guitar? It might cheer us all up.

TETEREV: [*equably*] My dear Akulina Ivanovna, I don't think providing you all with entertainment was an obligation of my lodging here.

AKULINA: [*missing what he said*] I'm sorry . . . ?

TETEREV: So am I.

BESSEMENOV: [*annoyed and taken aback*] I just don't understand you, Terenty Khrisanfovich. If you don't mind me saying so, you're a layabout and a drifter, and yet you spend your whole life behaving as if you're the lord of the manor. May I ask why?

TETEREV: That's the way I am, I'm afraid.

BESSEMENOV: Just what is it you've got that you're so bloody proud of?

AKULINA: There isn't much for a man like *him* to be proud of. He's just showing off.

TATYANA: Mother!

AKULINA: [*jumps*] Oh dear, what is it now? Have I said something wrong again? I'll keep quiet, if that's what you want.

BESSEMENOV: That's right mother, keep quiet. We're among *educated* people now. Now they've got all that superior knowledge they can criticise whoever and whatever they please. We're too old. We're too stupid to understand anything.

AKULINA: [*smoothing things over*] Never mind. At least they've had an education.

PERCHIKHIN: You weren't lying, old friend. It may have been a joke but you were telling the absolute truth.

BESSEMENOV: It's no joke, my friend.

PERCHIKHIN: Well, whatever . . . it's true. Old people are stupid!

BESSEMENOV: Looking at you, I can see what you mean.

PERCHIKHIN: I don't count, I'm stupid anyway. No, I'd even go as far as to say that if there were no old people there'd

be no stupidity. We burn like damp wood when we
think; a lot of smoke and no fire.

TETEREV: You've never said a truer word.

[POLYA *looks tenderly at her father and lays a hand on
his shoulder.*]

BESSEMENOV: [*sullenly*] Have it your own way. Carry on with your
lies if you must.

[PYOTR *and* TATYANA *break off their conversation and watch* PERCHIKHIN, *amused.*]

PERCHIKHIN: [*enthusiastically*] Old people are stubborn, you see.
We know we're wrong, we know we don't under-
stand anything, but we won't admit it. We can't.
Pride. We think to ourselves, "Can I possibly have
lived all these years and worn out thirty pairs of
breeches and still don't know anything? Never! It's
too painful to contemplate." So we go on and on
shaking our fists and bellowing, "I'm old! I'm right!"
and that gets us nowhere because our brains have all
seized up. But the young are bright and they have
their wits about them.

BESSEMENOV: [*rudely*] And you're talking through your hat. If we're
so stupid, shouldn't we be taught some sense?

PERCHIKHIN: No point in that. Be like pissing in the wind.

BESSEMENOV: Wait a minute. Don't interrupt me. I'm older than
you are. What I'm saying's this: why is it that the
ones who have bright, sharp minds have to run away
from us and go and hide in a corner where they can
make faces at us and don't have to talk to us? You
think about that! And I'll go and do some thinking
too, on my own, since I'm too stupid for this
company.

[*He gets up from his chair noisily and goes to the door of
his room.*]

My clever children!

[*A pause.*]

PERCHIKHIN: [*to* PYOTR *and* TATYANA] Now look what you've done!
You've hurt the old boy's feelings.

POLYA: [*smiling*] It was you, father.

PERCHIKHIN: Me! I haven't offended anybody in my life!

AKULINA: Oh, dear God, what's wrong with us all? I don't like
this. Why did you all upset him? You've all got such
an inflated idea of yourselves. All this dissatis-

faction with the world. He's an old man and he needs a bit of peace and quiet. He needs a bit of respect. He's your father, after all. I'd better go and speak to him. Polya! You wash up the tea things.

TATYANA: [*going to the table*] Why is father so angry with us?

AKULINA: [*from the door*] Because, clever girl, you're always trying to avoid him.

> [POLYA *washes the dishes whilst* TETEREV *puts his elbows on the table and stares at her with heavy eyes.* PERCHIKHIN *goes over to* PYOTR *and sits down at the little table.* TATYANA *slowly makes her way to her room.*]

POLYA: [*to* TETEREV] Why are you staring at me like that?

TETEREV: No reason.

PERCHIKHIN: What are you thinking about, Pyotr?

PYOTR: How to get out of this place.

PERCHIKHIN: There's something I've been wanting to ask you for a long time. Would you tell me, please, exactly what is a sewerage system?

PYOTR: Why do you want to know? It's too boring really. It would take far too long for me to make you understand.

PERCHIKHIN: But you do *know* about these things, don't you?

PYOTR: Of course I do.

PERCHIKHIN: [*looking at* PYOTR *with disbelief*] Hmmm . . .

POLYA: I wonder what's keeping Nil Vasilyevich so long?

TETEREV: Your eyes are very beautiful.

POLYA: You said that yesterday.

TETEREV: And I'll say it again tororrow.

POLYA: Why will you?

TETEREV: I don't know. Perhaps you think I'm in love with you, or something like that.

POLYA: No, I don't. I don't think anything like that.

TETEREV: Don't you? Then think away.

POLYA: What am I supposed to think?

TETEREV: You can think whatever you like. What about thinking about why I keep saying things like this? Think it over and let me know what you think.

POLYA: You're a strange man.

TETEREV: So you keep telling me. And I'll keep telling you that you should get away from here. This house is bad for you.

PYOTR: I'm sorry, is this a declaration of love? Shall I leave the room?

TETEREV: Don't worry. I think of you as a piece of the furniture.

PYOTR: That's not very funny.

POLYA: [*to* TETEREV] Don't be a bully!

[TETEREV *walks away and listens attentively to what* PYOTR *and* PERCHIKHIN *are saying.* TATYANA *comes out of her room with a shawl wrapped round her. She sits at the piano and starts to leaf through some sheet music.*]

TATYANA: Is there any sign of Nil?

POLYA: No.

PERCHIKHIN: I wouldn't say this is the most cheerful house I know . . . Now, Pyotr, I read in the newspaper the other day that in England or somewhere like that they've built a flying boat. It looks like a boat but you sit in it and press a button and whooosh! It shoots straight up into the clouds and carries people heaven knows where. I'm told a lot of Englishmen have completely disappeared. What do you think, Pyotr, is it true?

PYOTR: Of course it isn't.

PERCHIKHIN: But it says so in the paper.

PYOTR: The papers are always printing rubbish like that.

PERCHIKHIN: Is that so?

[TATYANA *plays quietly: a sad tune.*]

PYOTR: [*annoyed*] Yes it is!

PERCHIKHIN: All right, all right. Don't be angry. I never understand why you youngsters are so snooty with us ancients. You don't seem to want to talk to us. I don't like it.

PYOTR: What next . . . ?

PERCHIKHIN: My departure, since you've had enough of me. Polya, when will you be coming home?

POLYA: When I've done the clearing up.

[POLYA *goes out.* TETEREV *follows her with his eyes.*]

PERCHIKHIN: We used to go catching tomtits together, Pyotr, have you forgotten? You were fond of me then, weren't you?

PYOTR: I'm still fond of you.

PERCHIKHIN: I can see how fond you are of me.

PYOTR: I was fond of honey-cake in those days. And lolli-pops. But I don't like them any more.

PERCHIKHIN: I see. [*to* TETEREV] Shall we go and have a beer?

TETEREV: I'm not in a drinking mood tonight.

PERCHIKHIN: Oh well, I shall just have to go on my own. They're simple folk there. It's cheerful and friendly. A man could die of misery here, and it's nothing you should be proud of. You don't seem to do anything. You don't seem to want anything. Why don't we have a little game of cards? There's four of us. Let's play for trumps.

[TETEREV *smiles at* PERCHIKHIN.]

You're not up to it? Suit yourself then. I'll be off.

[*He goes up to* TETEREV *and gestures knocking back a drink.*]

Coming?

TETEREV: No.

[PERCHIKHIN *gives a hopeless wave of his hand and goes out. Silence. We can hear the notes that* TATYANA *is picking out on the piano.* PYOTR, *who is lying on the couch, takes up the tune, whistling.* TETEREV *gets up from his chair and walks around the room. In the hall outside we can hear something iron being knocked over and* STEPANIDA's *voice saying: "Who in heaven's name brought you here?"*]

TATYANA: [*continues playing*] Why hasn't Nil come home?

PYOTR: Why doesn't anybody come?

TATYANA: Are you waiting for Yelena?

PYOTR: Anybody!

TETEREV: Why should anybody want to come and see you?

TATYANA: You're always so world-weary.

TETEREV: The reason why no one will come, is because you have nothing to offer.

PYOTR: Terenty-the-Wise has spoken.

TETEREV: [*remorselessly*] Have you noticed how that old soak of a bird-man is fully alive, heart and soul, whilst you two who are only on the threshold of life are nearly half-dead?

PYOTR: And you? How do you assess your own wonderful qualities?

TATYANA: [*getting up from the piano*] Oh, stop it. This has all been said before.

PYOTR: I like your style, Terenty Khrisanfovich. And I like your chosen role of Grand Inquisitor of the Household. But I don't know why it amuses you since you always sound as if you're administering the last rites.

TETEREV: You'll have to get a real priest to give you those.

PYOTR: Perhaps, but you don't like us, that's the real point, isn't it?

TETEREV: It's true. I don't.

PYOTR: Thank you for being so forthright.

[*POLYA comes in.*]

TETEREV: I'll drink to that!

POLYA: You'll drink to what?

TATYANA: To rudeness.

TETEREV: To forthrightness! The truth!

POLYA: I want to go to the theatre. Will somebody come with me?

TETEREV: Well, I'd be only too . . .

PYOTR: What's on?

POLYA: 'Second Youth'. Oh, do let's go, Tatyana Vasilyevna.

TATYANA: No thank you. I will not be going to the theatre this season. It's boring. I loathe all those dreadful melodramas with guns going off all the time and people wailing and sobbing.

[*TETEREV strikes a key with one finger on the piano and the room echoes with a rich, sad sound.*]

It's so artificial. Life batters us enough as it is without all that noise and shouting. And it does it without one even noticing . . . without any tears.

PYOTR: [*gloomily*] They give us all these plays about suffering and love, but nobody even notices when a man's soul is being torn apart because of his desires and his duty.

[*TETEREV smiles and continues to hit the bass notes.*]

POLYA: [*smiling self-consciously*] I love going to the theatre. I adore it. Think of Don Cezar de Bazan! Wonderful! He's my idea of a real hero.

TETEREV: Don't you think I'm rather like him?

POLYA: You! Go on! Not the slightest bit . . .

TETEREV: [*an ironic smile*] How sad.

TATYANA: When actors try to play love scenes on the stage it just makes me want to be sick. It's never like that in real life. Absolutely never.

POLYA: Well, I'm going. Are you coming, Terenty Khrisanfovich?

TETEREV: No, since you don't think I'm like the wonderful Spanish Grandee, I shall have to disappoint you.

[*POLYA goes out laughing.*]

PYOTR: Who is this Spanish character of hers?

TETEREV: She obviously finds something healthy and energetic in him.

TATYANA: And no doubt he dresses beautifully.

TETEREV: And he's jolly. Baddies are never good-natured.

PYOTR: In that case you must be the biggest scoundrel of all time.

TETEREV: [*coaxing rich, gentle sounds from the piano*] I'm just a drunk. No more than that. Do you know why there are so many drunks in our beloved Russia? Because drinking is the easy way. We Russians adore a drunk. We hate people who are bold and original, ah, but a drunkard — we love him! It's always so much easier to love trivial, worthless things than to love something great and good.

PYOTR: [*pacing the floor*] Our beloved Russia, doesn't it sound strange? Is it really ours? Mine? Yours? Who are we when we talk about 'we'?

TETEREV: [*sings*] "We—eeeee! Are free—eee . . . wingèd birds . . . !"

TATYANA: Terenty Khrisanfovich, please stop banging away like that. It sounds like a dead march.

TETEREV: [*continuing*] I'm only adding a little background music to reflect the prevailing atmosphere.

[*TATYANA, annoyed, sweeps out of the room.*]

PYOTR: I don't care, please stop it. It's getting on my nerves . . . It seems to me that when a Frenchman or an Englishman says 'France' or 'England' he has a clear, concrete understanding of what the word means. But when I say 'Russia' it seems just an empty sound. And I find myself incapable of giving the word any real significance.

[*Pause.* TETEREV *plays.*]

There are so many words we use by force of habit, without thinking about their real meaning. Take 'life' . . . 'my life' — how much meaning is crammed into those two words.

> [*He paces the floor in silence.* TETEREV *strikes the keys softly, filling the room with the plangent sounds of the strings and following all* PYOTR's *movements with a frozen smile on his face.*]

Why on earth did I let myself get involved in all those ridiculous student demonstrations? I went to the university to study and I was studying . . . stop that noise, for God's sake stop that hammering . . . I had no idea that the so-called 'regime' was preventing me from studying Roman Law, absolutely no idea at all. All I knew about was the demands of 'so-called' *comradeship* . . . and, stupidly, I gave into them. Two years of my life wiped out! *That's* oppression. Oppression against me. And I'd been thinking all that time that I'd finish university, become a lawyer, get a job, read a lot, study all the richness of life . . . I was really going to live!

TETEREV: [*a prayer, delivered ironically*] To the intense gratification of your parents, the church and the state as befits a humble servant of society . . .

PYOTR: Oh no, not society. I despise society. My so-called comrades were always screaming 'society' at me. It wants more and more from us but it never lets us look further than the horizon. "Be a responsible citizen. Stand up for your rights!" Well, I was a citizen, damn them. But I am not duty-bound to submit to whatever society wants. I'm an individual. I'm a free man. Will you please, finally, once and for all, *terminate that damned pounding on the piano!*

TETEREV: I'm accompanying the most respected young citizen . . . or should I say ex-citizen . . . ? How long did your citizenship last? Half an hour?

> [*A noise outside in the hall.*]

PYOTR: One day you'll go too far.

> [TETEREV *looks mockingly at* PYOTR *and continues pounding at the piano. Enter* NIL, *with* YELENA, SHISHKIN, TSVETAEVA *and* TATYANA *slightly behind.*]

YELENA: What an awful funeral dirge! Good evening, bogeyman. Good evening, not-quite-lawyer. What are you up to?

PYOTR: [*sullenly*] Nothing of any interest.

TETEREV: This man has unfortunately died before his time. So I was playing something appropriate.

NIL: Will you do something for me?
[*He whispers in* TETEREV's *ear.* TETEREV *nods.*]

TSVETAEVA: It was a wonderful rehearsal, so fascinating!

YELENA: Oh, Citizen Lawyer! You should have seen how Lieutenant Bykov threw himself all over me.

SHISHKIN: Don't worry, Bykov's just a puppy.

PYOTR: What makes you think I'm the least bit interested in your flirtations?

YELENA: What on earth's the matter with you?

TSVETAEVA: There's always something the matter with him.

SHISHKIN: Yes, it's the way he is, poor chap.

YELENA: Tanya! I suppose you're in one of your autumnal moods as well, are you?

TATYANA: As usual, yes.

YELENA: And I'm feeling on top of the world. Why am I always so happy?

NIL: An unanswerable question! I'm not going to try because I'm happy too.

TSVETAEVA: And me. So am I!

SHISHKIN: Well, I may not be happy *always* . . .

TATYANA: But you are *all the time*.

YELENA: Tanya! Was that a joke? Well done! Now tell me, bogeyman. Why am I so happy?

TETEREV: You are the very soul of Frivolity.

YELENA: Wha-aat? Very well, then. I'll remind you of that the next time you start trying to flirt with me.

NIL: I must have something to eat. I'm back to work soon.

TSVETAEVA: What, all through the night? You poor thing, you.

NIL: Oh yes, all through the dark night, hour after hour without rest . . . I think I'll go and see Stepanida and pay her my respects.

TATYANA: Don't worry, I'll speak to her for you . . .
[*She goes out with* NIL.]

TETEREV: Tell me now, quickly, has fate truly made it our destiny to fall in love? Am I enslaved for ever?

YELENA: Yes, you are, you rude man! Yes, you are, you bad-

TETEREV: [*stepping back*] Then I will, I must, tell you the truth! It must be said. I was once in love with two women! And a married lady! At the same time!

YELENA: [*creeping up on him threateningly*] And what happened?

TETEREV: Nothing happened! It was all, all in vain.

YELENA: [*under her breath, indicating* PYOTR] What was going on between the two of you?

[TETEREV *laughs. They chat quietly together.*]

SHISHKIN: [*to* PYOTR] Could you let me have a rouble for three days or so? Boots have split.

PYOTR: Go on. That's seven you owe me now.

SHISHKIN: I won't forget.

TSVETAEVA: Pyotr Vasilyevich, why don't you join in our plays?

PYOTR: I'm no good at acting

SHISHKIN: You don't think we're any better, do you?

TSVETAEVA: You ought to come to rehearsals. The soldiers are so sweet. There's one called Shirkov, he's so funny. He's very sweet and innocent, with a shy smile and so adorably bone-headed!

PYOTR: [*watching* YELENA *out of the corner of his eye*] I don't understand how you can be interested in anyone who's stupid.

SHISHKIN: Shirkov's not the only one . . .

PYOTR: Oh, I'm sure they're all as bad as each other.

TSVETAEVA: I don't know how you can say such things. Why are you so unpleasant? Is it snobbery?

TETEREV: [*suddenly speaking out loud*] I'm incapable of feeling pity!

YELENA: Shhh!

PYOTR: I'm middle-class. You know that.

SHISHKIN: Which is why I can't understand your attitude to the common people.

TETEREV: Who's ever pitied me?

YELENA: [*under her breath*] You should give good in return for evil.

TETEREV: What have I got to give? I haven't got a kopeck.

YELENA: Not so loud.

PYOTR: [*overhearing them*] I don't know why you should pretend to feel sympathy for the 'common people' when you don't.

TSVETAEVA: We're not pretending. We share whatever we can with them.

SHISHKIN: It's more than that. We enjoy their company. They're uncomplicated. It's a breath of fresh air. Like the air of the forests. We need to fill our lungs with fresh air from time to time.

PYOTR: [*insistently, suppressing his anger*] You're living in a dream world. I don't know what ulterior motives you have for pandering to these soldiers. I'm sorry if I'm being blunt but to look for some kind of spiritual regeneration amongst soldiers . . . is, if you don't mind me saying so . . .

TSVETAEVA: Not just the soldiers, we give performances at the railway depot as well . . .

PYOTR: What's the difference? All I'm saying is that you can run around in circles doing all these good works for some lofty ideal or other, but you're deceiving yourself if it ever changes anything. You think you're helping some poor soul to develop his individuality but tomorrow his officer or his foreman is going to come along and punch him on the head, and all the enlightenment that you think you've planted in his head, if you've managed to plant anything at all, is going to be knocked right out again.

TSVETAEVA: It makes me so depressed to hear that kind of nonsense.

SHISHKIN: It just makes me angry. It isn't the first time I've had to listen to it and every time I do, I like it less and less. One of these days, Pyotr, you and I are going to have a jolly good talk, once and for all.

PYOTR: [*a sarcastic drawl*] You terrify me. I just can't wait.

YELENA: Why do you pretend to be like this? [*to the others*] I don't know why he wants us all to think he's such a nasty bit of work.

PYOTR: Perhaps I'm just showing off.

TSVETAEVA: You are, you just want to be different. All men put it on in front of women. Some pretend to be nihilists and some try to behave like Mephistopheles. But you're all layabouts, the lot of you.

TETEREV: Spot on. Well said!

TSVETAEVA: Ah! You're fishing for compliments now, are you? Well, you'll have a long wait. I know you too well.

TETEREV: Which is more than I do. If you know so much,

maybe you can answer this one: should one return good in exchange for evil? That is to say, do you think they're worth the same?

TSVETAEVA: Oh, you're always making up creaky old paradoxes.

SHISHKIN: Hold on. Don't stop him. I always like hearing what Teterev's got to say. We always think such mundane thoughts but he'll sneak something unusual into our heads one way or another. Let him finish.

PYOTR: You're far too generous. I think you may be crediting others with your own virtues.

SHISHKIN: No, no, let's be fair. It doesn't hurt to face the truth occasionally. I've never said anything remotely original in my life. But I wish I could, I do so wish I could!

TETEREV: You've just done it.

SHISHKIN: What! Is that a joke? Do you mean that?

TETEREV: I do. You've just expressed something original. But I'll leave you to guess what it was.

SHISHKIN: It must have slipped out by chance.

TETEREV: It's difficult to be original on purpose. I've tried.

YELENA: Come on, then. Don't torment us. Tell us what you've got to say about good and evil.

SHISHKIN: Come on, let's hear you let off some real philosophical steam.

[TETEREV *strikes a pose. He begins his speech in quite a light vein, but he becomes more and more serious as he goes on, so that by the end he is speaking with a great deal of fervour.*]

TETEREV: Most respected bipeds! You're quite wrong when you say that one should return good for evil. Evil is something you were born with, so it isn't worth very much. Good is a thing that you have acquired at enormous expense; the rarest, most precious and most beautiful commodity on earth. And so I conclude that to return good for evil would be futile and would gain you absolutely nothing. Return good for good. And never give away more of it than you receive. Man is greedy; having got more than he needs the first time, he will want the same treatment the next time. But never give him less than he needs, for man never forgets an injury, and if you cheat him once he'll tell the whole world that you're bankrupt.

He will have lost his respect for you. The next time, instead of returning to you the good you deserve, he'll only give you charity. So always be scrupulous how you return good for good because the man who gives charity to his neighbour is the most hateful creature on this earth. But when you receive evil make sure you return it a hundred times over. Return your neighbour's evil with brutal generosity. If, when you ask him for bread he gives you a stone, you are quite justified, my friends, in bringing down on his head the entire mountain!

> [*There is an uncomfortable feeling as* TETEREV *turns away. Everyone is aware of his sincerity and the gravity with which he has spoken.*]

YELENA: [*gently*] You must have suffered a great deal at the hands of other people.

TETEREV: [*grinning*] Yes, but I haven't given up hoping that they'll be made to suffer too. Either *by* me or *for* me.

> [NIL *comes in with a bowl of soup. He is watching it carefully as he speaks, trying not to spill it.* TATYANA *is following him.*]

NIL: Tanya has a bad habit. She has this tendency to moralise over every tiny little thing. "It is raining." — a moral. "You have hurt your finger." — another moral. "The stove is belching out smoke." — a third. I can't help thinking that education isn't good for some people if it teaches them to turn every triviality into a philosophy.

TATYANA: You are so *rude*, Nil.

NIL: [*sitting at the table*] Am I? Look, if you're bored, why don't you do something? There's no time to be bored if you work. If you don't like living at home, go and live in the country. They need teachers there. Or go to Moscow and learn something there.

YELENA: Well said, Nil! [*indicating* TETEREV] And that one needs a good talking to as well.

NIL: [*giving him a quick glance*] Oh yes, another exhibit. The New Heraclitus.

TETEREV: The New Swift, if you don't mind.

NIL: Much too flattering.

PYOTR: I agree with that.

TETEREV: I rather liked the sound of it.

TSVETAEVA: What a cheek!

NIL: [*not looking up from his food*] Calm down, everybody. [*more diffidently*] Has Polya been here? Does anybody know where she's gone?

TATYANA: She's gone to the theatre. Why are you asking?

NIL: No reason. I just wanted to know.

TATYANA: Do you want her to do something for you?

NIL: No. That is, not at the moment. But, generally speaking . . . I always . . . want her. Hell! What am I saying . . . ?

[*They all smile, but not* TATYANA.]

TATYANA: [*insistently*] Tell me what you want her for.

[NIL *carries on eating and ignores the question.*]

YELENA: [*quickly, to* TATYANA] What was Nil taking you to task about? I'm dying to know.

TSVETAEVA: Oh, yes, come on! That should be interesting.

SHISHKIN: I like the way Nil puts someone in their place.

PYOTR: I like the way he eats, too.

NIL: Let's face it, I'm pretty good at most things.

YELENA: Come on now, Tanya. Tell us all about it.

TATYANA: I don't want to.

TSVETAEVA: She never wants to do anything.

TATYANA: How do you know? There might be something I want to do very much. I might want to die.

TSVETAEVA: That's horrible.

YELENA: [*shudders*] I hate it when people talk about death.

NIL: There's nothing to say about it, is there? Until you're dead.

TETEREV: Now that's what I call philosophy!

YELENA: Why don't we all go up to my room? The samovar must have boiled by now.

SHISHKIN: A glass of tea! That's just what I want. And a little something to go with it, perhaps.

YELENA: Of course!

SHISHKIN: [*indicating* NIL] I looked at him. I was green with envy. Look at me, I'm a poor miserable creature . . .

NIL: Well, you don't need to envy me any more because it's all gone, and since I've got an hour or two to spare, I'll come upstairs for some more.

TATYANA: You should really have a sleep before you go back to work.

NIL: No, I shouldn't.

YELENA: Pyotr, are you coming?

PYOTR: Yes. If that's all right.

YELENA: It will be a pleasure! Give me your arm!

TSVETAEVA: Everybody form pairs! Nil Vasilyevich, you're with me!

SHISHKIN: [*to* TATYANA] And you're with me.

TETEREV: They always say that there are more men than women in the world, but of all the towns I've ever lived in, I have never known a single one where there's been a woman left over for me.

[TATYANA *laughs. She makes for the door, singing as she goes.*]

TATYANA: "Allons enfants de la patri — i — i — i — e!"

SHISHKIN: [*giving* PYOTR *a shove in the back*] Come along, my enfant de la patrie!

[*They go out singing and laughing and making a lot of noise. For a few seconds the room remains empty. Then the door to* BESSEMENOV's *room opens and* AKULINA *comes out yawning and putting out the lamps. The old man's voice is heard inside the room as he recites his prayers in a droning voice. In the darkness* AKULINA *stumbles against chairs as she makes her way back to her room.*]

END OF ACT ONE

ACT TWO

The same.

An autumn day:noon. BESSEMENOV *is sitting at the table.* TATYANA *is slowly and silently pacing up and down.* PYOTR *is looking out of the window.*

BESSEMENOV: I've been talking for more than an hour, but nothing I say has any effect on you. One's got his back to me listening, and the other one's strutting up and down like a crow on a fence.

TATYANA: All right, I'll sit down.
[*She sits down.*]

PYOTR: [*turning round to face him*] Just tell us, straight-forwardly, what exactly it is you want.

BESSEMENOV: I simply don't know what kind of people I've brought into the world. I'm trying to find out what kind of a man you are.

PYOTR: Be patient. You'll find out sooner or later. I haven't even finished my studies yet.

BESSEMENOV: Go ahead and study, then. I'd be happy if you did, if it would stop you arguing and complaining about everything . . . It seems to me that all you've learned is contempt for everything that moves. You haven't learned a sense of proportion. They chucked you out and you don't think it was fair. Well, you're wrong. A student is there to learn things and not change the world. If every twenty-year-old with half a brain decided to become a law-maker, it would turn the world upside down and leave no ordinary people left to do anything. You've got to go out and learn, be good at what you do, and when you've done that you can split as many hairs as you like. Until that glorious day comes the world and his dog can tell you and your opinions to bugger off. I'm not looking to always find fault with you. I'm saying this from the bottom of my heart because you're my son, you're my own flesh and blood. I wouldn't say it to Nil even though he's my foster-son and you know I've had a struggle with him as well. But he's not the same blood as me. And the longer things go on, the more obvious it is. I know he's going to be no good, that one. He'll probably end up an actor or something like that. Or a Socialist! Too bad, he doesn't deserve any better.

AKULINA: [*peeping in at the door; plaintively*] Father! I think it's time for dinner, isn't it?

BESSEMENOV: Go away! Keep your nose out of this. It's none of your business.

[AKULINA *withdraws.* TATYANA *glances at her father, gets up and starts pacing the room again.*]

You see! Your mother doesn't get a moment's peace. She's on her guard day and night. She's terrified I'm going to hurt your feelings. I don't want to hurt anybody. But you've hurt *me*. And you've hurt me deeply. I have to creep around my own house as if the floor was covered with broken glass. My old friends have stopped coming to see me. They say, "We're afraid your children will laugh at simple folk like us, now they've become so educated." And you have laughed at them more than once. And it's made me blush with shame. You'd think that educated children were the plague the way my friends have dropped me. You behave as if your father didn't exist. You never say a kind word to me. You never tell me what's going on inside your head. You never tell me what you're planning to do. I'm a stranger. But even so . . . I love you! Love you! Do you understand what love means? All right, they chucked you out, but do you have to take it out on me? Tatyana's pining away about something and turning into an old maid in front of my eyes. I don't know what to say about it to anyone. Why is my Tanya any worse than the ones that get married? And I want to see you a man, Pyotr, not a student. Philip Nazarov's son has finished his studies, married a girl with a good dowry, gets two thousand a year *and* he's become a member of the council.

PYOTR: Be patient. I'll get married one day.

BESSEMENOV: Oh, you will, I'm sure you will. You'd get married tomorrow if you could. To that flighty little slag upstairs. And she's a widow! Oh dear, oh dear!

PYOTR: [*flaring up*] You have no right to call her that.

BESSEMENOV: Call her what? A widow? Or a slag?

TATYANA: Father! Please! Please stop this! Pyotr, either leave the room or shut up. That's what I'm trying to do, I'm trying to keep quiet. Father, I know that what you're saying is right. Please believe me, I feel for it and I feel for you. But your sense of right is different from Pyotr's and mine, don't you see? We have our own way of looking at things. Now, wait . . . don't get angry. There's more than one truth, father.

BESSEMENOV: [*jumping up*] You're lying! There's only one truth! My truth! Where is yours? Come on! I want to see it!

PYOTR: Don't shout, father. I agree with Tatyana. You're right but your truth is too narrow for us. We've outgrown it in the same sense that we've outgrown our clothes. It's stifling and it's weighing us down. I'm sorry, your orderly way of doing things simply isn't for us.

BESSEMENOV: So that's it. You're educated and I'm a fool.

TATYANA: No, father, it isn't like that.

BESSEMENOV: Yes, it is. When your friends come round here the place is pandemonium and nobody can get any sleep. [*to* PYOTR] You play around with that lodger of ours right in front of my eyes. [*to* TATYANA] And you spend your whole life mooning around. Your mother and I are shoved into a corner.

[AKULINA *bursts into the room, crying pitifully.*]

AKULINA: My darlings! I'd gladly stay in the corner, or out in the shed if only you'll stop fighting. As if I would . . . do I ever complain, husband? Oh, my darlings, stop it please, you're tearing each other to pieces!

BESSEMENOV: [*seems to pull her towards him with one arm and fight her off with the other*] Get out of here, you stupid woman. They don't need you. They don't need either of us. They're too clever. We're not their sort.

TATYANA: This is torture! I can't bear this torture!

PYOTR: [*white with frustration*] Can't you see how stupid this is, father? This has suddenly happened, out of the blue. It's stupid!

BESSEMENOV: Suddenly happened? No, this has been building up inside me for years.

AKULINA: Leave him alone, Petya! Don't argue. Tanya, try and understand your father.

BESSEMENOV: You say it's stupid. It isn't stupid. It's a tragedy. We've lived together all these years and now suddenly there are two truths. You two are nothing but animals!

TATYANA: Pyotr, you must go. Father, I beg you to calm down.

BESSEMENOV: Heartless beasts! Are you proud of squeezing us out? You've achieved absolutely nothing and us who have made a home for you, we've lived our life . . . and sinned as well. We've even sinned for you.

PYOTR: [*shouting*] Did I ever ask you to do it?

AKULINA: Pyotr, on my knees . . .

TATYANA: Get out of here, Pyotr! I can't stand it any longer. I must go away . . .

> [*She sinks exhausted into a chair.*]

BESSEMENOV: That's right, you run away from the truth like a virgin from a band of Cossacks! But you can't run away from your conscience.

> [NIL *flings the doors wide open. He has just come from work. His face is black with soot and his hands are filthy. He is wearing a short, belted jacket, shiny with grease, and dirty, knee-length boots.*]

NIL: [*holding out a hand*] Who's got twenty kopecks for the cab-driver? Quick!

> [*The suddenness of his arrival and his calm voice manages to quieten everyone. He realises what has been happening. He smiles.*]

What's going on here? Another family quarrel?

BESSEMENOV: [*shouts*] You bloody heathen! Where do you think you are?

NIL: I don't know. Where am I?

BESSEMENOV: Cap! Take off that cap!

AKULINA: It's too much! Bursting in here in that state. What are you going to think of next?

NIL: Come on. Somebody give me some money.

PYOTR: [*gives him some money; whispers*] Come back as quickly as you can!

NIL: Need help? Heavy going, is it? Shan't be a tick.

> [*He goes out.*]

BESSEMENOV: Look at him! Another one with a lot of half-baked ideas. Where in heaven's name does he pick them up from? He doesn't seem to have any respect for anything.

AKULINA: I know, I know. Rowdy! Impetuous! Tanya, go to the kitchen and tell Stepanida we're ready to eat.

[TATYANA *goes out.*]

BESSEMENOV: [*wryly, to* AKULINA] Where are you going to send Pyotr? I don't know, you daft old thing. Don't you understand that it isn't because I'm angry? I'm not a wild beast. I'm afraid. I'm afraid for them. I'm only crying out because there's a deep pain right down in my soul. Why do you keep spiriting them away from me?

AKULINA: I know, my dearest, I know. I can see how things are, but can't you see, I feel sorry for them? We're old and we're not much good for anything any more. But they've got their lives ahead of them. They're going to know unhappiness enough, poor things, without us adding to it.

PYOTR: You're getting worked up about nothing, father. You've just got one thing in your head . . .

BESSEMENOV: I'm afraid. I'm afraid of these times. They're no good for us. Everything's coming apart. There's nothing but chaos all over the place. That's why I'm afraid for you, because . . . [*Pause.*] I don't know what would happen if . . . Who would support your mother and I then? We haven't anyone else to lean on. You keep your eye on that Nil. You can see what he's up to. And Teterev too. They kick with the same foot those two. Keep out of their way because I warn you, they hate us.

PYOTR: That's ridiculous! What can possibly happen to me? If you'll just wait a little longer, I'm going to write to the university and ask them to reinstate me.

AKULINA: Do it soon, Petya, and put your father's mind at ease.

BESSEMENOV: It restores my faith in you, Pyotr, when I hear you talk sensibly and seriously like that. It reassures me that maybe you'll live your life no worse than me. But sometimes . . .

PYOTR: Let's leave it there, shall we? I've lost track of the number of times we've had this out.

AKULINA: You're very precious to me, my darlings.

BESSEMENOV: And what about Tatyana? Why doesn't she give up teaching? All it does is wear her out.

PYOTR: It's true, she needs a rest.

AKULINA: She does indeed.

[NIL *comes in. He has changed into a blue shirt, but he hasn't washed yet.*]

NIL: Any sign of dinner?

[*As soon as* NIL *arrives,* PYOTR *dodges out into the hall.*]

BESSEMENOV: You better wash your face before you start asking for food.

NIL: It won't take long to wash my face, it isn't that big, but my appetite's enormous. Last night nearly killed me, the old engine was on its last legs and the wind was so cold! I'd like to put the boss in that old locomotive and take him for a ride on a night like that.

BESSEMENOV: That's right, just carry on like that. I've noticed how you've been talking about your superiors recently. There'll be trouble, I can see it coming.

NIL: No, they won't be in any trouble, don't worry.

AKULINA: Father was talking about you, not your superiors.

NIL: About *me.* Was he?

BESSEMENOV: Yes, you.

NIL: Ah!

BESSEMENOV: None of your cheek. You listen to me!

NIL: I'm all ears.

BESSEMENOV: You're getting too full of yourself.

NIL: How long have I been like that?

BESSEMENOV: You see. And a sharp tongue too.

NIL: [*sticks his tongue out and tries to look at it*] Have I? Let me see . . .

AKULINA: [*shaking her head*] Shameless boy. Who do you think you're sticking your tongue out at?

BESSEMENOV: Don't interrupt, mother.

[AKULINA *shakes her head reproachfully and then goes out.*]

You think you're a smart young feller, don't you? I want a word with you.

NIL: After dinner?

BESSEMENOV: No. Now.

NIL: No, I think after dinner would be better. I'm very hungry and very tired and frozen to the marrow. So what about later? And in any case there isn't really much for you to say, is there? You want an argument and I don't. It would be better if you just came out with it and admitted you hated my guts.

BESSEMENOV: Why don't you go to the devil!

[BESSEMENOV *goes to his room and slams the door shut behind him.*]

NIL: [*quietly*] He'd be much better company than you.

[*He walks round the room, humming.* TATYANA *comes in.*]

Been having another row?

TATYANA: You can't imagine what it was like.

NIL: I can, perfectly. You were acting a dramatic scene from the long-running comedy 'Round and Round in Circles'.

TATYANA: It's easy for you to laugh. You always manage to keep out of it.

NIL: If you mean I know how to stay clear of all this endless worrying and fighting, yes, I do. And quite soon I shall be well away from it all. For ever. I'm sick to the teeth of driving rusty goods trains night after night. I wouldn't mind if they were express trains screaming through the night, but crawling along at the speed of an old snail, it's just boring. I want to work with other people. I'm transferring to the depot to be a fitter.

TATYANA: You want to get away from us.

NIL: I'm sorry to be blunt, but yes, I do. I like life! I like decent, hard work and good-natured, straightforward people. You don't live. You just hang onto life by the shirt-tails and complain endlessly, for no reason at all. I don't know what it is that's bothering you. It beats me.

TATYANA: Do you really not understand?

NIL: I really don't. If you were sleeping in an uncomfortable position you'd turn over. Well, if life's uncomfortable why can't you apply the same principle instead of lying there moaning about it?

TATYANA: Didn't the philosopher say that only fools found life simple?

NIL: Philosophers probably know a lot about that. I'm not setting myself up as an expert on the subject. Life here is interminable and deadly dull. You complain because you want something more out of it. Why bother? Nobody's listening and they couldn't help you if they were.

TATYANA: Where did you learn to be so hard, Nil?

NIL: That's being hard, is it?

TATYANA: Callous. It's something you've picked up from Teterev, who hates everybody for some reason.

NIL: He doesn't hate everyone. [*laughing*] Have you ever noticed how like an axe he looks?

TATYANA: An axe? What sort of axe?

NIL: You know, the ordinary kind. A steel one with a wooden handle.

TATYANA: Oh, stop making a joke of everything. It's quite unnecessary. I enjoy talking to you, of course, it's refreshing. But why do you behave so thoughtlessly?

NIL: How am I thoughtless?

TATYANA: With anybody. With me, for example.

NIL: Not anybody, then . . .

TATYANA: No! Not anybody. *Me.*

NIL: With you?

[*They both fall silent.* NIL *looks at his boots.* TATYANA *looks at him expectantly.*]

I like you. And I respect you.

[TATYANA *leans forward.*]

But I don't think you should be a schoolmistress. It's not right for you. It tires you out and makes you tense. I'm not saying it isn't an important job, because children are the people of the future. We must know how to understand them and love them. I suppose we have to love any job, to do it well. I like working with iron. It's a wonderful thing to hammer away at that red, shapeless mass when it's raging and burning. When it spits sizzling hot fire at you and tries to burn out your eyes and blind you. You hammer great blows down on this living breathing thing that's trying to jump out of your hands, and you can turn it into anything you like.

TATYANA: That takes a great deal of strength.

NIL: And skill too.

TATYANA: Don't you ever feel sorry for anybody, Nil?

NIL: Sorry for whom?

[YELENA *comes in.*]

YELENA: You haven't had dinner yet, have you? Right! You're coming to my room. I have just baked the most delicious pie. Where's the reluctant lawyer? I promise you, it's the pie of your dreams.

NIL: [*going to her*] Then it's a deal. I'll demolish your pie for you. I'm dying of hunger and they're deliberately not giving me any food. I seem to have annoyed them for some reason.

YELENA: I've no doubt it was something to do with that tongue of yours. Come on, Tanya.

TATYANA: I must tell mother.

[*She exits.*]

NIL: How did you know I stuck my tongue out at father?

YELENA: I had no idea. Did you? Oh, do tell me what happened.

NIL: No, you tell me about that pie of my dreams.

YELENA: I shall find out! As for the pie, I was given the recipe by a murderer. My husband let him help out in the kitchen. He was such a pitiful, thin little thing.

NIL: Your husband?

YELENA: Gracious no, my husband was over six foot tall.

NIL: A midget.

YELENA: Oh, be quiet. And he had whiskers like this. [*shows him*] Six inches on either side.

NIL: I've never heard of a man's whiskers being a mark of his virtue.

YELENA: Unfortunately his whiskers were the only good thing about him.

NIL: Sorry to hear it. But to get back to the pie . . .

YELENA: This particular prisoner was a chef who murdered his wife. I was very fond of him. He didn't really murder.her, you see . . .

NIL: I know, it was an accident.

YELENA: Oh, get away with you. I don't want to talk to you!

[TATYANA *appears in the doorway and watches them.* PYOTR *comes in from the other side.*]

Now, Mr. Lawyer! How would you like to come upstairs and sample my pie?

PYOTR: Very much.

NIL: His old man gave him a talking to for not showing respect.

PYOTR: Drop the subject.

NIL: I hope he isn't intending to join us without asking permission.

PYOTR: [*looks nervously into his parents' room*] Come on, if we're going.

TATYANA: You go. I'll join you in a minute.

> [NIL, PYOTR *and* YELENA *go out.* TATYANA *goes towards her room.*]

AKULINA: [*from her room*] Tatyana!

TATYANA: [*impatiently*] What is it?

AKULINA: [*appearing in the doorway*] Come here! [*whispers*] Has Petya gone up to that woman's room again?

TATYANA: Yes. And I'm going too.

AKULINA: More troubles. She'll get her claws into that boy. I know it's going to happen. Speak to him. Tell him he must keep away from her. Tell him she isn't good enough for him, please tell him! She has no more than three thousand to her name and that's including her husband's pension. I know it.

TATYANA: Don't bother about it. She isn't the slightest bit interested in Pyotr.

AKULINA: It's deliberate. Quite deliberate! That's what she acts like in front of you and me. But she's got her eye on him like a cat watching a bird, don't you worry.

TATYANA: Why should I care? It's nothing to do with me. Speak to him yourself and leave me alone. I'm tired, haven't you noticed?

AKULINA: You don't have to tell him now. Lie down and have a rest first.

TATYANA: [*almost shouting*] There isn't any rest. I'm already worn out for ever. For ever! I'm going to be tired for the rest of my life. Tired of you and tired of everything!

> [*She hurries out into the hall* AKULINA *makes to go after her. Then she clasps her hands despairingly and stays put, her mouth open.*]

BESSEMENOV: [*looking in*] What is it now?

AKULINA: Nothing. Tatyana was just . . .

BESSEMENOV: Just what? Answering back again?

AKULINA: [*hurriedly*] Oh no, nothing like that. I don't know what gave you that impression. I was just telling her that dinner was ready and she said she didn't want any, and so I was asking her why and she . . .

BESSEMENOV: You're lying.

AKULINA: It's God's truth, I swear it.

BESSEMENOV: How often do you tell lies for them? Come on, look me in the eye. You can't, can you? Oh dear, oh dear, oh dear.

> [AKULINA *stands in front of him, hanging her head. A pause.*]

We should never have had those two educated. It's built a brick wall between them and us.

AKULINA: [*quietly*] No, father, ordinary people aren't any better these days.

BESSEMENOV: We should never give children more than we got. It's hard for me to say it, but they haven't got any character, the pair of them. No backbone. We all ought to have something special. Nil's too cocky and he's a bad lot but he's got character. I wouldn't turn my back on him but at least you know what he's about. [*a heavy sigh*] When I was young I loved going mushroom-gathering and listening to the music in church. I haven't a clue what Pyotr's interested in.

AKULINA: He's with his lady friend upstairs again.

BESSEMENOV: Oh, is he! I'll show her a thing or two, you see!

> [TETEREV *comes in, looking even more heavy-eyed than normal. He has a bottle of vodka and a glass.*]

They let you loose with a bottle again, have they?

TETEREV: I started last night. When we'd got vespers out of the way.

BESSEMENOV: Why do you do it?

TETEREV: No reason. Will dinner be ready soon?

AKULINA: I'm just about to lay the table now.

> [*She starts to busy herself.*]

BESSEMENOV: It seems such a waste. You're quite a sensible sort of man, Terenty Khrisanfovich. Why are you destroying yourself with vodka?

TETEREV: Most honourable *bourgeois*, you are wrong. It isn't the

vodka that's destroying me. It's too much pent-up
energy. Too much energy, that's my downfall.

BESSEMENOV: You can't have too much energy.

TETEREV: You're wrong again. No-one needs it these days. All
you need is low cunning; the agility of a snake. [*turns
back a sleeve and tenses a muscle*] I could smash that table
with one blow. But what can I use an arm like this for
today? I can use it to chop wood with. But writing
with it would be a waste, wouldn't it? Stupid. So
what can I do with my strength? I suppose the best
thing to do would be to join a circus and exhibit
myself in a side show, lifting weights and breaking
iron chains. But I was a good student once. I was
even bright enough to get thrown out of theological
college. I'm an educated man and I don't want to be
on display in a circus so that people can come and
gawp at me in dumb amazement.

BESSEMENOV: You're a dangerous man.

TETEREV: Animals my size are never dangerous; you don't
know your zoology. Nature is much more subtle
than that. If I was as fierce as I am strong, you'd
never be able to escape me.

BESSEMENOV: Why would I want to run away? I'm in my own
house.

AKULINA: Don't listen to him, father.

TETEREV: Quite right, you're in your own house, oh honourable *bourgeois*. But your house is everywhere and
that's why there's nowhere for me to live.

BESSEMENOV: You're chucking your life away. You're not doing
anything with it. You could do if you wanted to.

TETEREV: I don't want to. I loathe all that. It's a much nobler
occupation to get drunk and bring about my own
ruin than it is to live and work for your kind. Can you
really see me, sober and neatly dressed, deferring to
you like one of your servants? Of course you can't.

[POLYA *comes in but when she sees* TETEREV *she
draws back.* TETEREV *grins and shakes his head. He
holds a hand out to her.*]

Hello! Don't worry, I shan't talk to you like that
again. I know everything!

POLYA: [*confused*] What! You couldn't know.

AKULINA: Here you are! Go and tell Stepanida to bring the soup in.

[POLYA *goes out.*]

BESSEMENOV: About time too. [*to* TETEREV] I like listening to you reason things out, especially when it's about yourself. You certainly look terrifying enough. But even when you're sounding off about this and that, I can still see all your weaknesses.

TETEREV: You're a model *bourgeois*. That must be why I like you. You're a bit wise and a bit stupid, a bit good and a bit not so good, a bit honest and a bit devious, a bit brave and a bit of a coward; and the embodiment of everything that's not worth bothering about. You are the great force of ordinariness which vanquishes everything in its path and lives for ever in triumph. Let's drink a toast in cabbage soup, oh worthy mole!

BESSEMENOV: We will when they deign to bring it in. But I can't understand why you're so argumentative. You don't need to hurt people's feelings deliberately. I believe in talking things over quietly and sensibly, so that people will be only too pleased to listen. Who wants to hear insults? Fools might, I suppose.

[NIL *comes in.*]

NIL: Has anyone seen Polya?

TETEREV: [*with a smirk*] Yes.

AKULINA: What do you want her for?

NIL: [*going over to* TETEREV] At it again. You seem to be doing a lot of that at the moment.

TETEREV: It's better than drinking blood. Human blood's got so thin and stale recently, hasn't it? It's really not as rich as it used to be It's all been sucked dry.

[POLYA *and* STEPANIDA *come in,* STEPANIDA *with a tureen and* POLYA *with a plate of meat.*]

NIL: [*going to* POLYA] Hello. Are you going to give me an answer?

POLYA: [*in an undertone*] Not here. Not in front of everyone.

NIL: I don't see why not. There's nobody here to be afraid of.

BESSEMENOV: What are you talking about?

NIL: Me. And her.

AKULINA: What's going on?

BESSEMENOV: I don't know what's going on.

TETEREV: [*laughs and pours some vodka*] I do.

BESSEMENOV: What is this all about? Pelagea?

POLYA: [*embarrassed*] Nothing.

NIL: [*sitting down*] It's a secret. A dark secret.

BESSEMENOV: Oh well, if it's a secret you can nip off into the corner and share it there. Are you trying to make fools of us? I don't know what I'm doing in my own house sometimes. Whispering and gesturing and plotting in corners. And I'm supposed to sit here like the village idiot with my mouth open. Who in heaven's name do you think I am?

AKULINA: I've got to agree with your father, Nil.

NIL: [*calmly*] Foster-father. There's no reason to get overexcited and turn this into a drama. It isn't anything out of the ordinary.

POLYA: [*gets up again from her chair*] Nil . . . Vasilyevich . . . made me . . . I mean, told me . . . no, asked me . . .

BESSEMENOV: Come on!

NIL: Don't try and frighten her. I only asked her, if maybe, you know, she might like to marry me.

> [BESSEMENOV's *spoon remains suspended in mid-air as he stares incredulously at* NIL *and* POLYA. AKULINA *is thunderstruck.* TETEREV *stares ahead, heavy-eyed. His hand twitches.* POLYA *looks down at the table.*]

She told me she'd give me her answer today. That was her answer.

TETEREV: [*with a wave of the hand*] You see. It was simple.

BESSEMENOV: It was certainly simple. [*bitterly*] But then that's how things are done nowadays. So there's nothing more to say, is there?

AKULINA: How could you be so brutal? What were you thinking about? Couldn't you have talked to us about it first?

NIL: [*annoyed*] Damn! I knew I shouldn't have mentioned it.

BESSEMENOV: Mother! Say nothing. Shut your mouth and get on with your food and I'll do the same. It's nothing to do with us.

TETEREV: [*sounding drunk*] Well, I've got something to say. No, maybe I'd better not.

BESSEMENOV: All of us had better not. Though I'd like to say, after all I've done for you, it's a miserable reward. It's just like you to go behind my back.

NIL: I've worked hard to pay for my keep, and I'll carry on doing it, but you can't force me to do what you want. You wanted to marry me off to that silly Sedova woman, just because she had a dowry of ten thousand roubles. I don't want her. I love Polya. I've loved her for a long time and I haven't exactly been keeping it a secret. I've always been open and I always will be. You've got nothing to reproach me with.

BESSEMENOV: [*restraining himself*] All right. Go ahead and get married. I'm going to stop you. But I'd like to know what you're going to live on . . . if it isn't a *secret*.

NIL: We'll work. I'm getting transferred to the depot. And she . . . well, she won't have any difficulty finding something. Don't worry about your thirty roubles a month.

BESSEMENOV: Time will tell, won't it?

NIL: Would you like it in writing?

TETEREV: Now then, honourable *bourgeois*, make sure you get a written guarantee. Go on.

BESSEMENOV: You keep out of this.

AKULINA: You're a fine one to give advice.

TETEREV: No, go on! Make him! I don't think you can. I think you're too soft. I don't think you've got the courage. Nil, write him out a piece of paper that says, "I take it upon myself every calendar month to pay . . . "

BESSEMENOV: I can do that if I want to. He's had food and clothes and shoes to put on his feet since he was ten. He's twenty-seven now.

NIL: Why don't we settle our accounts later?

BESSEMENOV: If that's what you want. [*flaring up*] But just remember one thing. You and me are enemies from now on. This is an insult I'll never forget. Never.

NIL: An insult? How have I insulted you? You weren't hoping I was going to marry *you*, were you?

BESSEMENOV: [*doesn't hear*] I won't forget. Stabbing me in the back when I'd fed and clothed you. All in secret, never asking my advice. [*to* POLYA] And you! So quiet and

humble there. What are you staring at the table for?
Cat got your tongue? What I could do to you . . .

NIL: You can't do anything to her. Stop bellowing. This is
my house too. I've handed over my wages to you for
the last ten years. The man who works is the master
here too.

[POLYA *gets up and goes out during this. She meets*
PYOTR *and* TATYANA. PYOTR *glances in and disap-*
pears. TATYANA *stands holding on to the door-frame.*]

BESSEMENOV: [*stares at* NIL *dumbstruck*] Wha — a — a — at! You! The
master here!

AKULINA: We must go, father. We must go. [*shakes her fist at* NIL]
You'll get what you deserve, sooner or later. [*tear-*
fully] You wait!

NIL: The working man is always the master. It's about
time you began to realise it.

AKULINA: [*dragging* BESSEMENOV *out*] Come on! Let's leave
them. Not another word. Don't shout any more.
They won't listen to us, anyway.

BESSEMENOV: [*giving in to her*] You try and be the master. We'll see
who's the master here, if you do. We'll soon see that.

[BESSEMENOV *and* AKULINA *go to their room.* NIL
begins to pace. A barrel-organ can be heard outside.]

NIL: Well, that's livened things up a bit. What a bloody
fool I am. I should have kept my mouth shut.
Problem is, I can't keep anything to myself. It just
spills out.

TETEREV: That's not a bad thing. It was an extremely interesting performance. I enjoyed every minute of it.
You're quite good at playing heroic parts, so don't
worry. And believe me, at the moment, we need
heroes. We certainly do. In our age there are only
two sorts. The heroes — fools, in other words. And
the villains who are, I'm afraid, the clever ones.

NIL: I shouldn't have involved Polya in all this. That
terrible scene must have terrified her. No. She
doesn't frighten easily. Probably furious with me.
Ayeee!

[*When* TATYANA *hears* POLYA*'s name, she moves into*
the room. The barrel-organ can no longer be heard.]

TETEREV: It's a neat idea to divide the world up like that.

There are plenty of villains around too. They live on their wits and the only thing they know is that power is strength. Not my kind of strength, not the one in this chest and these arms, but the strength that comes from cunning. That's the mentality of a wild animal.

NIL: [*not listening*] The wedding will have to be soon. Too bad, we'll go ahead with it. I haven't had an answer, but I know what it's going to be, bless her. I despise that man so much. And this house. The life here is disintegrating. They're all freaks. They can't see how they've messed things up. They can't see that they're swimming in triviality. They've made their home into a prison and sentenced themselves to hard labour. I do not know how they managed it, but I don't respect them for it. I don't respect people who deliberately make a mess of their lives.

> [TATYANA *stops herself coming any further. She goes quietly to the trunk in the corner and sinks down onto it. She hunches herself up on it and seems even more small and pathetic.*]

TETEREV: Still, I suppose the fools make life interesting. There aren't many of them so I suppose we ought to value them. And astonishingly enough they seem to be altruistic. Always thinking up schemes for universal happiness and that sort of thing. Trying to find out what makes the world go round. Very foolish really, I suppose . . .

NIL: [*thoughtlessly*] Yes, I'm the foolish one. She's the one that's got her head screwed on. She loves life as well, but it's such a calm, sensible sort of love. I think we'll have a good life together. We're not afraid to take chances. We can achieve anything we set out to do. Oh, we'll manage . . . She's as innocent and open as a child. [*laughs*] We'll get along all right together!

TETEREV: A fool is a man who spends his whole life trying to work out what makes glass transparent, while a villain will come along and make a bottle out of it.

> [*The barrel-organ starts up again, but very close this time, almost under the window.*]

NIL: You never think of anything else but bottles.

TETEREV: Wrong. I never think of anything else but fools. A fool is the kind of man who wonders where the fire is before it comes to life and where it goes to when it's been put out. A villain just draws a chair up in front of it and keeps warm.

NIL: [*distantly*] Warm . . .

TETEREV: They're both fools in fact. But one is beautiful and heroic and the other is a useless beggar. And they both end up in the grave. It always ends up there! [*He laughs.* TATYANA *shakes her head, silently.*]

NIL: [*to* TETEREV] Are you all right?

TETEREV: I'm only laughing. The fools who are still alive look down on their dead brother and wonder where he's gone. But the villains just take over his estate and make sure they remain well-off until it's their turn. [*He laughs again.*]

NIL: You're well away, my friend, aren't you? Hadn't you better go to your room?

TETEREV: My room? Do I have a room?

NIL: Stop all this now. Do you want me to give you a hand?

TETEREV: You can't help me, comrade. I'm not on one side or the other. I'm not one of the accusers and I'm not one of the accused. I am a class on my own. Here is the material evidence of the crime. Life has been ruined, it's too small for real people. It doesn't fit. The philistines have trimmed it, and hemmed it in, and now it's too tight. That's the material evidence. Look at me! A decent man. I've no room to stretch. I've no reason and no excuse to live!

NIL: Come on now, old friend. Come on.

TETEREV: Let go of me. You think I'm going to fall, don't you? Don't be silly. I fell a long time ago. It's strange but I was just picking up the pieces again when along you came, and without knowing it, you knocked me over again. Never mind. We'll just keep going. You keep at it. You're strong and healthy. You can go where you like. You can do what you like. And because, because . . . I've fallen . . . I will watch you . . . with a look of approval and say . . . go on!

NIL: What are you on about? It sounds quite interest-
           ing . . . if I could understand a word of it.

TETEREV: I advise you not to try. Not necessary. Better not to
           understand everything. Some things. Do you no
           good. Just keep going. All right? Go on . . .

NIL: All right. I will go.

           [*He goes out, not seeing* TATYANA, *who is pressed into
           the corner.*]

TETEREV: [*bowing to him*] Robber, I wish you luck. You've stolen
           my last hope and you never realised it. To hell with it
           all!

           [*He goes to the table for his bottle, and notices the figure
           of* TATYANA *huddled up in the corner.*]
           Hello? Who's this?

TATYANA: [*softly*] It's me.

           [*The barrel-organ breaks off.*]

TETEREV: You. I thought it was a ghost.

TATYANA: No. Only me.

TETEREV: I can see that. But what are you doing there?

TATYANA: [*softly but clearly*] Because I have nowhere that I can
           run to, and nothing to make me carry on living.

           [TETEREV *goes up to her, quietly.*]
           I don't know what makes me so tired and depressed.
           But believe me, that's how I feel and I'm so desper-
           ately unhappy. I am only twenty-eight years old. I
           am so ashamed that I'm like this. So weak and
           pathetic. Inside me, where my heart should be
           burning, there's nothing but a void; it's all dried up
           and burnt out and yet it hurts so much. This empti-
           ness has overwhelmed my spirit and I don't know
           how it happened. [*Pause*]. I don't know why I'm
           telling you this.

TETEREV: I'm sorry. I don't understand . . . what you're
           saying. I'm too drunk. I don't understand a word of
           it.

TATYANA: Nobody ever talks to me the way I want them to. The
           way I always dreamed they would. I thought *he*
           would. I was patient and I waited, and in between,
           quarrels, pettiness — stifling me, crushing me,
           wearing me down. I didn't see what was happening.
           Now I don't have the strength to carry on living. No

strength, not even in the depth of my unhappiness.
I'm frightened. Now. I'm very frightened . . .

[TETEREV *shakes his head. He goes to the door and
opens it.*]

TETEREV: [*drunk*] A curse on this house! Curse it!

[TATYANA *goes to her room, slowly. The stage is
empty. A silence.* POLYA *enters, followed by* NIL. *They
go to the windows and* NIL *takes her by the hand.*]

NIL: [*quietly*] I'm so sorry for what happened. It was
unpleasant and unnecessary. I can't keep my mouth
shut when there's something I want to say.

POLYA: [*almost in a whisper*] It's all right. They don't mean
anything to me. It really doesn't matter any more.

NIL: I know you love me. I can see it. I won't ask you to
tell me. You're so funny. Last night you said, "I'll let
you know tomorrow. I've got to think it over." What
is there to think over? You love me, don't you?

POLYA: Of course I do. I've loved you for a long time.

[TATYANA *creeps out of her room and stands there listening.*]

NIL: We'll have a wonderful life together, just wait and
see! You're a good comrade, you look on the bright
side when things get tough, you're not scared of
going without things . . .

POLYA: Why should I be scared with you? I'm not a meek
person, I'm quiet that's all.

NIL: Yes, and stubborn. You're so strong. I've never seen
anything get you down. So! . . . I'm very happy. I
knew this would happen. I'm more happy than I've
ever been in my life.

POLYA: I knew it would happen too.

NIL: Did you? Really! That's wonderful. Don't you think
this is the best possible world to be alive in?

POLYA: Oh, my dear friend, my wonderful man, it is . . .

NIL: Say that again. It was like music.

POLYA: No more flattery. We ought to go. Someone might
come in. Come on.

NIL: Let 'em.

POLYA: No, no. We must. Oh go on, kiss me again.

[*They kiss, then* POLYA *breaks away from* NIL *and runs
out, past* TATYANA *without seeing her.* NIL *follows*

> *looking beatific, but notices* TATYANA *and stops in front of her. He is surprised and angry. She stares at him silently. Her eyes are blank, and she has a little twisted smile on her face.*]

NIL: [*with contempt*] You were listening! Were you watching us? I don't believe it . . .

> [TATYANA *stands very still, as if she's been turned to stone.* NIL *leaves the door open as he goes.* BESSE-MENOV's *rough voice can be heard shouting, "Stepanida! Who's spilt the coal? Do you know anything about this? Come and clear it up!"*]

END OF ACT TWO

ACT THREE

The same.

Morning. STEPANIDA *is dusting.* AKULINA *is washing the tea-things.*

AKULINA: There isn't much fat on the beef today, so you'd better take the fat from yesterday's joint and put it in the soup. That'll make it a bit richer. Are you listening to me?

STEPANIDA: Yes.

AKULINA: And when you cook that veal, don't put so much butter in the pan. I bought five pounds on Wednesday and when I looked yesterday there wasn't much more than a pound there.

STEPANIDA: Must have used it.

AKULINA: I know it's been used! You've put more on your head than a peasant uses to grease the wheels of a cart.

STEPANIDA: That's lamp oil. You ought to know the smell by now.

AKULINA: I know it all right! [*Pause.*] Where did Tatyana send you this morning?

STEPANIDA: To the chemists. She wanted some ammonia. Twenty kopecks' worth.

AKULINA: Another headache. [*sighs*] There's always something wrong with that girl.

STEPANIDA: Get her married off. That'd restore her to health and beauty.

AKULINA: It's not as easy as you think. You can't just marry a girl off these days. If she's got an education it's ten times worse.

STEPANIDA: Why don't you give a decent dowry? You'd soon shift her then.

[PYOTR *looks in through the door.*]

AKULINA: No. I'll never live to see the happy day. She doesn't want to get married.

STEPANIDA: Oh, doesn't she! At her age, she does.

AKULINA: Oh, dear. [*Slight pause.*] So who was paying court to madam upstairs last night?

STEPANIDA: The schoolteacher. Him with the red hair.

AKULINA: I know. The one whose wife ran off.

STEPANIDA: That's him. And the one that works in the tax office. Skinny one with a yellow face.

AKULINA: Oh, yes. Married to Pimenov's niece. He's a consumptive.

STEPANIDA: I'm not surprised. He looks like one.

AKULINA: Was our choirboy there?

STEPANIDA: Yes, him. He was warbling away until the early morning. Roaring like a bull! And Pyotr Vasilyevich . . .

AKULINA: When did Pyotr come back?

STEPANIDA: It was dawn when I opened the door for him.

AKULINA: [*shaking her head*] I don't know what . . .

[PYOTR *comes in.*]

PYOTR: Stepanida! Hurry up with what you're doing and get out of here, will you?

STEPANIDA: Won't be long. Sooner it's done, happier I'll be.

PYOTR: You'd be quicker if you didn't talk all the time.

[STEPANIDA *snorts indignantly and goes out.*]

Mother, I've told you over and over again not to gossip with her. It's appalling, discussing private things with the cook!

AKULINA: Who am I supposed to talk to? If my son won't talk to me, I might at least be allowed to talk to the cook.

PYOTR: You can't talk to her on equal terms. All you'll hear is a lot of malicious gossip.

AKULINA: I don't hear anything from you. You've been home for six months and the time you've spent with me doesn't add up to more than an hour. I'm still waiting to hear about your time in Moscow.

PYOTR: Will you listen . . .

AKULINA: And when you do deign to speak to me, it's only to tell me not to do something. You treat me like a silly girl — finding fault and making fun of me.

[PYOTR *makes a dismissive gesture and goes out into the hall.*]

That's what I mean! That was a nice long conversation!

[*She sobs and wipes her eyes on her apron.* PERCHI-KHIN *comes in. He is wearing a torn quilted jacket,*

*with bits of the padding sticking out of the holes in it
and tied at the waist with string, 'bast' clogs and a fur
hat.*]

PERCHIKHIN: Oh dear, what terrible troubles have we here? Pyotr
upset you? He flew past me. Not a word of hello. Is
my little Polya here?

AKULINA: [*sighs*] In the kitchen. Chopping up cabbage.

PERCHIKHIN: I'll tell you something. Birds go about things the
right way. Once the little chicks have got their
feathers they just fly off and go their own sweet way.
No marching and drilling needed from the parents
before they go. Any chance of a little drop of tea?

AKULINA: Yes. So you've taken up the day-to-day habits of the
birds yourself, have you?

PERCHIKHIN: Absolutely! I have! What could be better! I don't own
anything and I don't disturb anyone. I'm not down
on the ground, I live up in the air, you see.

AKULINA: [*with contempt*] That's why nobody respects you.
Here, drink this. It isn't very strong and it's cold.

PERCHIKHIN: [*raising his glass to the light*] No, it isn't strong, but I
can't take it too strong so let's be thankful for small
mercies. As for respect, don't you worry. I don't
respect anybody in any case.

AKULINA: Who needs your respect? I can't imagine.

PERCHIKHIN: And a jolly good thing too. This is what I think —
people who get their daily bread on earth only
snatch it from some other poor soul's mouth. But
my manna comes from the air! The birds feed me.
What could be finer! What could be more honest!

AKULINA: So. When is the wedding taking place?

PERCHIKHIN: Whose wedding? Am I getting married? Oh no, the
little songbird who's destined for yours truly hasn't
flown into my neck of the woods yet. I rather fear
she's a bit too late now . . .

AKULINA: Stop that nonsense and tell me when the wedding is.

PERCHIKHIN: Whose wedding?

AKULINA: Your daughter's! You know what I'm talking about.

PERCHIKHIN: My daughter? She can get married whenever she
wants. As long as she's got a husband, of course . . .

AKULINA: Did they plan all this a long time ago?

PERCHIKHIN: Did who plan what a long time ago?

AKULINA: Stop playing the village idiot. She must have told you.

PERCHIKHIN: Told me what?

AKULINA: About the wedding.

PERCHIKHIN: Whose wedding?

AKULINA: Damn you, you stupid old man! You ought to be ashamed of yourself behaving so stupidly.

PERCHIKHIN: Just a minute, just a minute. Be calm and tell me what all this is about.

AKULINA: I don't want to talk to you.

PERCHIKHIN: You have been talking to me. For a long time. And you've been getting nowhere.

AKULINA: [*tersely, with a note of bitterness*] When are you thinking of marrying your daughter Pelagea to Nil?

PERCHIKHIN: [*jumping up*] Polya and Nil!

AKULINA: Are you trying to tell me she hasn't told you? Her own father!

PERCHIKHIN: [*joyfully*] Is it true! You're having me on, aren't you? Nil? Well, bless them, bless them! The little devils! My little Polka! Not just a Polka now, we can have a whole quadrille! You're sure this isn't a joke? I can't believe it. And I was thinking all this time that Nil would marry Tatyana! I swear I did. It looked obvious to me.

AKULINA: Do you think we would let Tatyana marry that parasite? He's no use to us.

PERCHIKHIN: No use! You must be mad! If I had ten daughters I'd give every one of them to him without a second thought. Nil? He could feed a hundred mouths if he wanted to. Nil!

AKULINA: What a father-in-law Nil's getting! That's what I think when I look at you.

PERCHIKHIN: Father-in-law! [*laughs*] He won't have to worry about me. This bird-man's no burden! Watch me! See! The old legs are dancing on their own. I'm free as a bird! It's off to the woods for me. Nobody's going to see much of me. Poor little Polya. I used to worry about her and feel ashamed for her. I brought her into this life, but what could I do for her? But now . . . I can go wherever I want. I can go looking for the magic firebird!

AKULINA: You can't just pack up and go and leave everything behind. Now you've had some luck you don't want to run away from it.

PERCHIKHIN: But that's what my luck is! Being able to run away. She'll be happy. My Polya will be happy with that happy, healthy, kind-hearted chap. I'm singing for joy inside this old head and in here . . . [*points to his chest*] . . . there are little larks going . . . [*stamps his foot and whistles*] Now Polya's caught herself a Nil! All the birds will trill, will trill!

> [BESSEMENOV *comes in. He is wearing an overcoat and carrying his cap.*]

BESSEMENOV: Drunk again!

PERCHIKHIN: Drunk with happiness! Have you heard about Polya! [*laughs gaily*] She's going to marry Nil! Isn't that wonderful?

BESSEMENOV: [*unmoved*] It's nothing to do with us, is it? We've got what we deserved, no doubt.

PERCHIKHIN: And all this time I was convinced Nil had set his heart on marrying Tatyana.

BESSEMENOV: What's that you say?

PERCHIKHIN: I did really! Well, anyone could see that Tatyana wasn't, how shall I say, exactly against the idea. The little looks she'd give him. A nod here and a wink there, that kind of thing, if you know what I mean. And then! Right out of the blue!

BESSEMENOV: [*tightly*] I've only one thing to say to you. You might get away with things because you're a fool, but you don't say things like that about a decent young woman. That's the first thing. [*beginning to raise his voice*] The second thing. As far as your daughter goes I don't care what kind of a girl she is or who she makes eyes at, or if he bothers to return the favour. But if she marries Nil, that's the end of them, they're not worth a candle. I spit on them, even if they are up to their ears in debt to me. And now the last thing. Look at you! You may be a distant relative of mine, but what in heaven's name do you think you look like? A tramp. What made you think you could come dancing into my parlour in that disgusting state, with those rags and those old clogs, eh?

PERCHIKHIN: I beg your pardon? What are you saying, Vasily Vasilyevich? I always dress like this.

BESSEMENOV: I don't know how many times you've been here looking like that. All that matters to me is that you've obviously no respect for the master of this house! What do you think you are? A beggar? A vagrant? A bit of worthless riff-raff? Get out of my house! That's all I want to say! Get out!

PERCHIKHIN: [*devastated*] Vasily Vasilyevich! Why? What have I done?

BESSEMENOV: Don't pretend you don't know. Get out!

PERCHIKHIN: Now, just a minute, please. Think . . . I would never do anything . . .

BESSEMENOV: Go on. What are you waiting for? Get out before I throw you out!

PERCHIKHIN: [*going out; there is a note of pity in his reproach*] Shame on you, you foolish old man! It makes me sad to see you behaving like this. I'm sorry for you, I am truly. Goodbye to you.

> [BESSEMENOV *straightens himself up and paces the floor slowly, with measured steps. He looks intimidating.* AKULINA *carries on with the dishes but looks furtively at him from time to time. She is muttering and her hands appear to be trembling.*]

BESSEMENOV: What are you doing? Casting a spell?

AKULINA: Praying, praying . . .

BESSEMENOV: I'm not going to be mayor *now*, am I? It doesn't look at all likely. Thanks to them. Damn them!

AKULINA: What! Why ever not? Oh, now surely . . .

BESSEMENOV: You think surely, do you? There's Fedya Dosekin after the job now. That jumped-up little so-and-so who's head of the locksmiths' guild. He's still wet behind the ears.

AKULINA: Now don't lose heart. They haven't elected him yet.

BESSEMENOV: They will. They'll elect him. When I got there today he was sitting in the office sounding off about everything under the sun. "These are hard times," says he, "and we must help each other out. We've got to stick together, us master craftsmen. We can't afford to do things on our own with all these factories shooting up all over the place," says he. So I said, "It's the Jews. They're to blame for it all. They're the ones that should be kept in check!" I told him, "We should write to the Governor and tell him exactly how they're pushing us Russians out. Tell him to send them off to another country."

[TATYANA *opens the door and walks unsteadily towards her room.*]

And he smiled at me and said, "What about the Russians that are worse than the Jews?" Started making little remarks which I took to be directed at me. I pretended not to notice, of course, but I knew what he meant. I let the bastard drag on but I was thinking all the time, "You wait, I'll pin your ears back one of these days." And then! A bit later, Mikhail Kryukov, the stove-maker, comes up to me and starts suggesting that this rat Dosekin should be the mayor! He couldn't look me in the eye, but I thought, "Judas", the shifty little bastard.

[YELENA *comes in.*]

YELENA: Good morning, Vasily Vasilyevich. Good morning, Akulina Ivanovna

BESSEMENOV: Oh, it's you, is it? Come in. What can I do for you?

YELENA: I've come to pay the rent.

BESSEMENOV: [*managing to be more civil*] Oh, good, yes. How much have we got here? Twenty-five roubles? That leaves forty kopecks for the two panes of glass in the passageway. Then there's the lock on the wood-shed that your cook broke, we'll call that twenty kopecks.

YELENA: As precise as ever. I'm afraid I've no change. So I'll have to give you three roubles.

AKULINA: You've had a sack of coal too. Your cook had it from me.

BESSEMENOV: How much is it?

AKULINA: Thirty-five a sack.

BESSEMENOV: That makes ninety-five kopecks. Two roubles and five kopecks change. As you say, as precise as ever, my dear lady. It's being precise that keeps the world on an even keel. The sun rises and sets precisely when it should. So if everything in heaven's just so, there's all the more reason for it to be so on earth. Take yourself. You always bring your rent money on time.

YELENA: I don't like being in debt.

BESSEMENOV: That's very commendable. That way we all trust
                        you.
YELENA: Goodbye. I must go.
BESSEMENOV: My respects to you.
                        [*He watches her as she goes out.*]
                        Good-looking woman, damn her. Nevertheless, it
                        would still give me the greatest pleasure to kick her
                        out of here.
AKULINA: That wouldn't be a bad idea at all, father.
BESSEMENOV: On the other hand, we can keep an eye on her if she's
                        living upstairs. If she moves somewhere else then
                        Pyotr will end up hanging around there and if we're
                        not on the scene she'll get her way with him sooner
                        or later. And we can't ignore she's regular with the
                        rent and more than willing to pay for breakages.
                        Mind you, this is a dangerous business with Pyotr,
                        very dangerous . . .
AKULINA: I'm sure he doesn't want to marry her. He's only
                        after a bit of . . .
BESSEMENOV: If we could be sure of that, we could rest easy and
                        there's no more to be said. It's better if he does all
                        that at home, rather than hang about in brothels all
                        the time.
                        [*A hoarse, grating sob can suddenly be heard from*
                        TATYANA's *room.*]
AKULINA: [*quietly*] Did you hear that?
BESSEMENOV: What is it?
AKULINA: [*looking round anxiously*] Out in the hall, was it?
BESSEMENOV: Must have been the cat . . .
AKULINA: [*diffidently*] There was something I wanted to talk to
                        you about, father.
BESSEMENOV: Out with it then.
AKULINA: Do you think you might have been a bit hard on old
                        Perchikhin? The silly old fool doesn't mean any
                        harm . . .
BESSEMENOV: If he doesn't mean any harm, he won't take offence,
                        will he? And if he does, it's no loss to us. I don't
                        consider his acquaintance anything we should feel
                        honoured about.
                        [*The moan again, louder.*]
                        What *is* that, mother?
AKULINA: I don't know. What on earth is it?

[BESSEMENOV *rushes into* PYOTR's *room.*]

BESSEMENOV: Anybody here? Pyotr?

AKULINA: [*running after him in horror*] Petya! Petya! Petya!

TATYANA: [*calling out hoarsely from her room*] Help me! Mother! Save me! Save me!

[BESSEMENOV *and* AKULINA *run out of* PYOTR's *room and go towards the source of the noise. They hesitate at the door. Then they both push it and go in.* TATYANA's *cries can be heard more clearly.*]

[*off*] It's burning! It hurts! Oh! A drink! Give me a drink! Save me!

AKULINA: [*running out of the room, goes to the hall door*] Help! Someone please help! Petya!

BESSEMENOV: [*off*] What is it, daughter? What is it? What's the matter, my darling?

TATYANA: [*off*] Water! I'm dying! I'm burning inside! Oh, God.

AKULINA: [*looking off*] In here! Hurry! Please!

BESSEMENOV: [*off*] Get the doctor!

[PYOTR *runs in.*]

PYOTR: What is it? What's going on?

AKULINA: [*grasping him by the arm*] It's Tanya! She's dying!

PYOTR: [*pulling away*] Get off me! Get off me!

[TETEREV *comes in, pulling on his jacket.* PYOTR *goes into* TATYANA's *room.*]

TETEREV: What's the matter? Is there a fire?

BESSEMENOV: [*off*] Go and fetch the doctor, Pyotr! Tell him I'll give him twenty-five roubles.

[PYOTR *rushes out again.*]

PYOTR: [*to* TETEREV] Get the doctor! Tell him it's poisoning! Liquid ammonia, a woman, a young woman. Quickly! Quickly!

[TETEREV *runs out.* STEPANIDA *rushes in.*]

STEPANIDA: Oh my goodness, my goodness!

TATYANA: [*off*] Petya! I'm burning inside! I'm dying! I want to live! To live! Get me some water!

PYOTR: [*off*] How much did you take? When did you take it? Tell me!

BESSEMENOV: [*off*] My little daughter! My Tanechka!

AKULINA: My little dove! How could you do such a thing!

PYOTR: [*off*] Go away, mother! Stepanida, take her out! Go on! Go away!

[YELENA *runs into* TATYANA's *room.*]

Please take mother outside.

> [*An* OLD WOMAN *comes in from outside. She stands in the doorway, surveying the scene and muttering to herself.* YELENA *leads* AKULINA *gently out by the arm.*]

YELENA: [*a whisper*] It's all right. There's no danger.

AKULINA: My poor little dove, my baby daughter. What have I done, what have I done to you . . . ?

YELENA: It'll pass. The doctor will put everything right when he comes. This is dreadful!

OLD WOMAN: [*taking* AKULINA's *other arm*] Don't let it upset you, mother. What's happened, eh? She sick, is she? Is that all? Old Sitanov the merchant had his side half kicked in by a horse the other day.

AKULINA: My darling child! What am I going to do! You're my only one!

> [*They lead her out. In* TATYANA's *room her moans mingle with* BESSEMENOV's *gruff voice and* PYOTR's *nervous, unfinished phrases. There is a clattering of dishes and the sound of the iron bed being moved. A chair is knocked over and a pillow thuds to the floor.* STEPANIDA *runs in and out several times with her hair dishevelled, her eyes staring and her mouth hanging open, grabbing a cup or a plate from the sideboard and occasionally breaking one.*
>
> *Now faces appear from time to time at the hall door, but nobody dares to come in. A* YOUNG BOY, *a housepainter's apprentice, does come in and peeps into* TATYANA's *room. He runs back and announces in a loud whisper, "She's dying, she is!" The barrel-organ again, but this time quickly silenced. A buzz of conversation from the people in the hall: "He killed her!" . . . "Who?" "Her father!" "He said to her, 'You better be careful, young lady!' " "On the head!" "What with?" "No, no! She cut her own throat." A woman asks, "Was she married?" Some sympathetic noises. The* OLD WOMAN *comes out of* BESSEMENOV's *room and lifts some bread from the table as she passes and shoves it under her shawl. She goes to the door.*]

OLD WOMAN: Shh! She's on the way out!

MAN: [*off*] What's her name?

OLD WOMAN: Lizaveta.

WOMAN: [*off*] What did she do it for?

OLD WOMAN: It all started on Assumption Day. He says to her, "Lizaveta," he says . . .

> [*What sounds like a movement in the crowd.* TETEREV *comes in with the* DOCTOR. *Still wearing his hat and overcoat, he goes in to* TATYANA's *room.* TETEREV *glances in, then walks away, frowning. There is still a confusion of voices, noises and groans coming from the room. Meanwhile,* AKULINA's *wails can be heard from* BESSEMENOV's *room. She is shouting, "Let me go!", "Let me go to her!" There is still a muffled murmuring from out in the hall and the odd phrase, "That serious chap", "The choirsinger?", "That's him", "The one from St. John's".* TETEREV *makes for the door.*]

TETEREV: What are you doing in here? Go on! Get out of here!

OLD WOMAN: [*now fussing in the doorway herself*] Go along now, good people! It's none of your business.

TETEREV: Who are you? What are you after?

OLD WOMAN: I sell vegetables, sir. Spring onions, cucumbers . . .

TETEREV: So what are you doing here?

OLD WOMAN: I was on my way to visit Semyagina. She's god-mother to my children.

TETEREV: That still doesn't explain what you're doing here.

OLD WOMAN: I was just passing the door. There was a lot of noise, wasn't there? Thought there was a fire.

TETEREV: So . . .

OLD WOMAN: I just looked in. Came to see what all the trouble was.

TETEREV: Get out of here. All of you. Get out of this hallway!

> [STEPANIDA *runs out of* TATYANA's *room.*]

STEPANIDA: [*to* TETEREV] Go and fetch a bucket of water. Quick!

> [*An* OLD MAN, *with his face tied up in a handkerchief, looks in at the door and, with a wink, says to* TETEREV, *"Hey, mister, she pinched a bread roll off your table here!"* TETEREV *goes out through the hall, pushing people out of the way. A lot of noise and confusion. A boy cries out, "ouch!" and somebody else laughs. Somebody says reproachfully, "Not so loud!"*]

TETEREV: [*in the hall*] Off you go! Quick march!

PYOTR: [*looking out*] Quietly! [*turns back into the room*] Father, you'd better go to mother. Go on. [*calls out into the hall*] Don't let anyone in.

[BESSEMENOV *comes out, unsteadily. He sits down on a chair by the table and stares blankly in front of him. Then he gets up and goes into his room.* AKULINA*'s voice can be heard as he opens the door.*]

AKULINA: [*off*] Nobody could say I didn't love her! Nobody could say I didn't look after her!

YELENA: [*off*] Be calm, my dear.

AKULINA: [*off*] Father! Oh father, what is it . . . ?

[*Her speech is cut off as the door is closed. The room is now empty but noise filters through from two directions: the sound of voices in the* BESSEMENOVS' *room, and a whispered conversation, groans and movements from* TATYANA*'s.* TETEREV *brings in the bucket and puts it down by the door. He taps on it cautiously.* STEPANIDA *comes out, wiping sweat from her forehead.*]

TETEREV: Well?

STEPANIDA: Looks like everything's going to be all right.

TETEREV: Did the doctor say that?

STEPANIDA: Yes, but . . . [*waves her hand disparagingly*] He says we're not to let her mother or her father in.

TETEREV: Is she better, then?

STEPANIDA: Who knows? She's not groaning any more. She's gone green and her eyes are the size of saucers. Lying still, like a corpse. [*reproachful whisper*] I told them, heaven knows how many times . . . Get that girl a husband. A husband's what she needs. They didn't listen to me, and now this happens. It's not healthy for a girl to go on all this time without a husband. She doesn't believe in God either! She says, "Don't start praying and crossing yourselves" . . . *I* don't know!

[YELENA *comes in.*]

YELENA: How is she?

TETEREV: I'm not sure. I've heard the doctor thinks there's no danger.

YELENA: Her folks are in a dreadful state. I feel so sorry for them.

[TETEREV *shrugs but doesn't comment.*]

STEPANIDA: [*running out*] Oh, Lord! I forgot the stove!

YELENA: Why did she do it? What happened? Poor Tatyana! It must have hurt so much. [*screws up her face and shudders*] It must have done, don't you think? It must have been agony.

TETEREV: I don't know. Liquid ammonia's not one of the ones I've tried.

YELENA: This isn't a time for jokes.

TETEREV: I wasn't joking.

YELENA: [*goes up to the door of* PYOTR's *room and looks in*] And Pyotr? Is Pyotr Vasilyevich still in there with her?

TETEREV: He would be, wouldn't he, if he hasn't come out?

YELENA: Poor Pyotr, he must be so upset! [*Pause.*] If anything like that happens I always . . . sometimes I have a feeling of such disgust when I'm confronted by other people's misfortune.

TETEREV: [*smiling*] I admire you for that.

YELENA: Do you understand what I mean? I feel like taking it and stamping on it, and trampling it into the ground until it disappears.

TETEREV: You'd do that to misfortune, would you?

YELENA: Oh yes, I'm not afraid of it. I hate it. I want life to be happy and I want to have people around me all the time and be always doing something new. I know how to make life good for myself and for those around me.

TETEREV: Even better!

YELENA: Let me tell you, I can be quite hard. I don't like being around people who are always unfortunate. Some people are like that whatever you do for them. If you tear a man's hat off his head and let him feel the sun on it, however beautiful it feels, some people will still stumble about complaining, "Alas, miserable creature that I am! Ah me! All alone in the world! Ignored! Life is boring! Life is dreary! Oooooh! Aaaaah! Oooooh!" When I meet people like that, I'm usually overcome by an overwhelming desire to make them even more wretched.

TETEREV: Well said! I must confess I hate listening to women philosophising but when I listen to you, I could kiss your hand.

YELENA: [*flirtatiously*] Only my hand? And only when I'm

being serious? Oh dear, here I am fooling about and
being frivolous when someone in there is suffering.

TETEREV: [*indicating* BESSEMENOV's *door*] And in there as well.
You can't move for suffering people. It's habit-
forming, you know.

YELENA: But people really do suffer.

TETEREV: People do, yes.

YELENA: So we pity them, don't we?

TETEREV: It's better to help them than to pity them.

YELENA: You can't help the whole world, can you? And you
can't help anyone unless you pity them first.

TETEREV: Suffering is only the result of desire. But there's
desire that is worthy of respect and desire that is
unworthy of it. We should be helped to satisfy only
desires that make us healthy and strong and raise us
above the animals.

YELENA: [*not getting his drift*] Perhaps . . . What *is* going on in
there? Is she asleep? It's very quiet. I can hear whispering. The old folks are hiding themselves away too.
This is all so strange. One minute noise and confusion and groaning and shouting, the next it's all as
quiet as the . . .

TETEREV: That's life. People shout a lot, then they have a rest.
And then when they've had a rest, they start
shouting again. In this house everything comes and
goes quickly — shouts of pain or shouts of joy,
they're soon dissipated, like sound carrying across a
lake. The final echo here is always the echo of the
commonplace, which reigneth supreme. Triviality!
Whether it's rage or triumph that little household
god always has the last word here.

YELENA: I had a lot more fun when I lived in the prison. My
husband was always either drunk or gambling or
away hunting. It was miles from anywhere and there
were hardly any neighbours. I didn't go out
anywhere or get any invitations so I had a great deal
of time on my hands. I spent most of it with the
prisoners. They liked me. If you looked closely, of
course, you could see what an odd bunch they were
but they were also incredibly kind and uncomplicated. When I looked at them I found it hard to
believe that this one, for example, was a murderer or

this one was a thief, or somebody else had done some terrible thing. I once asked one, "Did you kill someone?" — "Yes, I did, Yelena Nikolayevna, I'm afraid I did. Nothing I can do about that." But it seemed to me that he wasn't any more guilty than any of us. He was only a stone that someone else had picked up and thrown away. I bought them books and made sure the cells all had draughts sets and playing cards. And I gave them tobacco and wine, only a drop, of course. They were just like children! They played ball and skittles when they were exercising. I used to read to them sometimes from funny magazines and make them roar with laughter. I bought songbirds and every cell had a cage in it. They loved those birds almost as much as they loved me! They liked me to dress in bright colours and so of course I did. [*sighs*] I had a good time with them. Three years just passed, like that, and when my husband was killed by a horse, I wept, not so much for him but because I would have to leave the prison and all my friends. I was so upset when I left and the prisoners were heartbroken [*looks around*] I'm not so happy here, in this town. And there's something unpleasant about this house. It's not really the people, but . . . oh dear, all this has made me feel wretched and depressed. We're chattering away here, and next door, in that room, a woman may even be dying.

TETEREV: [*serenely*] And we're not sorry.

YELENA: [*quickly*] Are you not?

TETEREV: Well, are you?

YELENA: [*softly*] No. I'm not. That sounds awful, but I'm not sure whether it is. Sometimes, you can see that something is terrible, but you can't feel it. It's odd but I feel more sorry for him, for Pyotr. I always have done. He has had such a hard time of it in this house.

TETEREV: Haven't we all?

[POLYA *comes in.*]

POLYA: Hello.

YELENA: [*going to her quickly*] Shh! Be quiet. Didn't they tell you? Tatyana has tried to poison herself!

POLYA: *What?*

YELENA: Yes, really. The doctor's in there too, and Pyotr.

POLYA: Is she dying? Will she die?

YELENA: We don't know.

POLYA: But why? Did she say?

YELENA: We don't know. She didn't say anything.

PYOTR: [*pokes a rather dishevelled head round the door*] Yelena Nikolayevna . . . could you come here a minute?
[YELENA *hurries in.*]

POLYA: [*to* TETEREV] Why are you looking at me like that?

TETEREV: How many times have you asked me that?

POLYA: What do you expect? If you keep looking at me like that. [*goes over to him*] You think this is all my fault, do you?

TETEREV: [*grinning*] Why? Do you feel guilty about it?

POLYA: The only thing I feel at the moment is that I like you less and less. Tell me how this happened?

TETEREV: She took a bit of a knock yesterday. Being a sickly creature she simply fell over. That's all there is to it.

POLYA: That isn't true.

TETEREV: What isn't true?

POLYA: I know exactly what you're trying to say. It's not true. Nil . . .

TETEREV: Ah! Nil! How does Nil come into all this . . . ?

POLYA: He doesn't. It isn't my fault and it isn't his. I know you want to blame us, but we couldn't have done anything. We love each other and we have done for a long time.

TETEREV: [*becoming more serious*] I don't blame you in the least. You've already humped up all that guilt on your shoulders and you're already trying to load it onto the first person you meet. Why? I have a great deal of respect for you. Didn't I spend hours nagging you and telling you to run away from this house as quickly as you could? I could see that it was unhealthy. I could see that it eats away the spirit. I was the one who kept telling you.

POLYA: So, what of it?

TETEREV: Nothing. Simply that if you had done what I said, you wouldn't have had to go through all this. That's all.

POLYA: Yes, but what made her do something like this? Is it really serious? What did she take?

TETEREV: Don't know.

> [PYOTR *and the* DOCTOR *come out of* TATYANA's *room.*]

PYOTR: Polya, will you go and help Yelena?

TETEREV: [*to* PYOTR] What's happening?

DOCTOR: Not too serious, I think. In fact if the patient wasn't so nervous and highly strung there wouldn't be much harm done at all. She didn't take very much. There are a few burns to the oesophagus. Some of it got into her stomach but she vomited it straight back up again.

PYOTR: Sit down. You must be tired.

DOCTOR: I'm obliged to you. She won't feel too good for a week or so. Not as bad as the one I had the other day. House-painter. Mistook a glass of varnish for a glass of beer . . .

> [BESSEMENOV *comes in. He stands in the doorway of his room and gives the* DOCTOR *a doom-laden look.*]

PYOTR: It's all right. She isn't in any danger.

DOCTOR: Absolutely not. She'll be up and about again in two or three days.

BESSEMENOV: Do you mean it?

DOCTOR: Certainly.

BESSEMENOV: Well, if you mean it, and there's no danger — thank you kindly. Pyotr, would you . . . come over here a minute?

> [PYOTR *goes over to* BESSEMENOV *and the two go into* BESSEMENOV's *room from which there is a murmuring and clinking of money.*]

TETEREV: [*to the* DOCTOR] What happened to the house-painter?

DOCTOR: I beg your pardon?

TETEREV: The house-painter you mentioned. What happened?

DOCTOR: Oh, him. Nothing at all. He recovered. [*looks at* TETEREV] We've met before, haven't we?

TETEREV: It's possible.

DOCTOR: Were you in hospital once? With typhoid.

TETEREV: I was, yes.

DOCTOR: [*pleased*] There you are! I never forget a face. Now . . . wasn't it in the spring? What is your name? It's coming to me . . .

TETEREV: Yes, I remember *you* now.

DOCTOR: There you are . . .

TETEREV: Yes. When I was getting better and I asked you if
              you'd increase my food rations, you puckered up
              that ugly little face of yours and said, "Be grateful for
              what you're getting. There are plenty of tramps and
              drunks like you outside."

DOCTOR: [*nonplussed*] What! But that's . . . What is your name
              now? . . . I am Dr. Nikolai Troyerukov. And you
              are . . .

TETEREV: [*going up to him*] I am Terenty the Wise, the incor-
              rigible drunkard, Custodian-of-the-Magic-Bottle!
                  [*The* DOCTOR *backs away from him*]
              Don't worry, I won't hurt you.
                  [*He walks past the* DOCTOR *into the hall. The*
                  DOCTOR *gives him a disbelieving look and fans himself
                  with his hat.* PYOTR *enters.*]

DOCTOR: [*glancing at the door into the hall*] All the same, I must be
              on my way. I have to make another call. If she com-
              plains of any pain, then repeat the dose. Just one or
              two drops, but it shouldn't be necessary. Good day
              to you. By the way, there was a very strange man in
              here just now. Is he a relative?

PYOTR: No, he's a lodger.

DOCTOR: He's quite a character. Very amusing. Good day to
              you . . . and thank you!
                  [*He goes out.* PYOTR *accompanies him into the hall.*
                  BESSEMENOV *and* AKULINA *come out of their room
                  and tiptoe cautiously over to the door of* TATYANA's
                  room.]

BESSEMENOV: Wait. Don't go in. Can't hear. Maybe she's having a
              sleep. Mustn't disturb her. [*takes* AKULINA *over to the
              trunk in the corner*] Well, mother, this has certainly
              been our red-letter day, hasn't it? Think of all the
              endless talk and gossip. It'll be all over the town . . .

AKULINA: Now then, father! What does it matter? They can
              shout it from the rooftops if they want. As long as
              she doesn't die. What do we care if they tell the
              whole town?

BESSEMENOV: I know. You're right. But . . . dear, oh dear . . . can't
              you understand? It's a terrible disgrace, this.

AKULINA: Disgrace? What's a disgrace?

BESSEMENOV: Our daughter's tried to poison herself! Imagine the

things people are going to say. What did we do to
her? How did we upset her? We must be beasts to
have driven her to it. They can all go to hell, of
course! I'll put up with anything for my children. All
I want to know is, why? They never tell me anything.
What's going on inside them? I don't know, I just
don't know.

AKULINA: I don't know either and I'm their mother. I run
around after them all day and never get a word of
thanks. I wouldn't mind as long as they were fit and
well, but when all this happens . . .

[POLYA *comes out of* TATYANA's *room.*]

POLYA: She's going to sleep now. We'd better keep our
voices down.

BESSEMENOV: How is she now? Can we go in to see her?

AKULINA: Just father and me. We'll be ever so quiet.

POLYA: The doctor said not.

BESSEMENOV: [*suspiciously*] How do you know? You weren't there
when the doctor came.

POLYA: Yelena Nicolayevna told me.

BESSEMENOV: Oh, *she's* in there, is she? Hear that? Complete strangers can wander in and out but not her own mother
and father.

AKULINA: I suppose we'll have to take our meals in the kitchen
so we don't disturb her. Poor darling, we're not even
allowed to take a peep at her now.

[AKULINA *makes a despairing gesture and goes out.*
POLYA *is leaning against the sideboard and staring at
the door into* TATYANA's *room. She is frowning and
tight-lipped and is standing very stiffly.* BESSEMENOV
sits at the table as if waiting for something.]

POLYA: [*quietly*] Has my father been here today?

BESSEMENOV: I don't know why you're asking me about your
father. You're not trying to tell me you care about
him, are you? I know who you care about.

[POLYA *looks surprised.*]

Yes, he was here. In his usual filthy state and
behaving worse than ever. But you should respect
him! He's your father.

POLYA: I do respect him. I don't understand what you're
saying.

BESSEMENOV: I'm saying it for your benefit. He's a tramp and he's barely got a roof over his head. But never mind, you be sure and respect him! Not that you know what being a father means. You've got no feelings, you young ones. Look at you, you've got no money and nowhere to live and yet you go around having opinions about this and that as if you had an education. Have you no humility, girl? You're going to get married now and there's a woman in there who nearly killed herself . . .

POLYA: What are you saying? I don't understand you.

BESSEMENOV: [*lost*] Well, try. Have a think about it. I'm only trying to make you understand that you're nothing. And you're getting married and my daughter . . . What are you hanging about for? Go into the kitchen and make yourself useful. Go on!

[POLYA *stares at him, then begins to leave.*]

Just a minute! I shouted at your father . . .

POLYA: Why?

BESSEMENOV: That's nothing to do with you. Go on . . .

[POLYA *goes out, confused.* BESSEMENOV *tries to peep into* TATYANA's *room.* YELENA *comes out and drives him out.*]

YELENA: Don't go in. You'll disturb her. She's sleeping.

BESSEMENOV: You can disturb us as much as you like, but we can't disturb you, is that it?

YELENA: [*taken aback*] What do you mean? She's ill.

BESSEMENOV: I know, I know . . .

[*He goes out into the hall.* YELENA *watches him leave and shrugs. She sits on the couch. She puts her hands behind her head, closes her eyes and smiles dreamily.* PYOTR *comes in, looking depressed and dishevelled. He moves his head as if trying to shake free of something. He sees* YELENA *and stops.* YELENA *doesn't open her eyes.*]

YELENA: Who's that?

PYOTR: Why are you smiling? It's a bit strange to see someone smiling after . . .

YELENA: [*glancing at him*] You're in a bad mood. And tired, you poor boy. I feel so sorry for you.

PYOTR: [*sitting beside her*] I feel sorry for myself.

YELENA: You should go away.

PYOTR: I know. What am I doing here? I'm sick to death of it.

YELENA: What kind of life do you really want? I keep asking you that but you never tell me.

PYOTR: It's difficult for me to say.

YELENA: Even to me?

PYOTR: Especially to you. I don't know what you think of me. I don't know how you'd react if I did tell you. But I do think sometimes that you . . .

YELENA: That I what?

PYOTR: That you . . .

YELENA: That I like you? Of course I do. Very much. You're a dear, sweet boy!

PYOTR: [*heatedly*] I'm not a boy! I can think for myself. I want to know what you think about Nil and Shishkin and Tsvetaeva, and all that idealistic group of do-gooders. Do you like it when they start spouting quotations from all these worthy books and putting on plays for the workers? Is all this philanthropy any use? Do you think we should live like that? I want an honest answer.

YELENA: Darling, I just can't say, you know I'm the most ignorant person in the world. And probably the most frivolous too. I like them because they're lively and they're always doing something. I like cheerful people — that's how I am. Why do you ask?

PYOTR: Because they bother me. I don't mind if living like that makes them happy. I don't mind if they want to believe that everything they do is so important. I wouldn't interfere with that, if they didn't interfere with my life, and call me cowardly and egotistical and things like that.

YELENA: [*touching his hand*] You're tired, you've had a hard time.

PYOTR: I'm not tired, I'm angry. Can't I live the way I choose to live? It's my right, isn't it?

YELENA: [*playing with his hair*] That's much too deep a question for me to answer. I live the way I choose to and nobody is going to persuade me to go to a nunnery. If I was made to, I'd simply run away or throw myself in the river.

PYOTR: Well, you've spent more time with that lot than I

have, and you obviously like them, I can see that,
but . . . as far as I can see, they're all empty vessels.

YELENA: What!

PYOTR: Empty vessels. Make the loudest sound . . .

YELENA: Oh, yes. But what about me? I'm an empty vessel if
ever there was one.

PYOTR: No, no! You're full of life. You're as clear and as cool
and as invigorating as a spring deep in the forest!

YELENA: Brrr! I sound terribly cold!

PYOTR: No! This isn't funny. It's important! Don't laugh! Am
I that amusing? I want to live. With my own free will
I want to live the life I've planned for myself.

YELENA: Go on, then! What's stopping you?

PYOTR: Whenever I make the decision a voice keeps telling
me I must not.

YELENA: What? Your conscience?

PYOTR: No! Not my conscience. I'm not about to do
anything criminal, am I?

YELENA: [bending over him] That isn't what you want to say at
all, is it? There's a much simpler way of putting it.
Poor boy! I think I'll have to help you or you'll tie
yourself up in knots about something which is so
easy.

PYOTR: Yelena Nicolayevna! Don't laugh at me. I'm trying to
be as straightforward as I can . . .

YELENA: And that's not the way either!

PYOTR: I'm so weak. I can't manage life at all. I know how
trivial and futile this atmosphere is. But what can I
do to change it? I want to go away. I want to be indep-
endent.

YELENA: [taking his head in her hands] Repeat after me, "I
. . . love . . . you." Go on, say it.

PYOTR: Oh, I do, I do! But you're making fun of me again.

YELENA: Far from it. I'm deadly serious. I made up my mind a
long time ago to marry you. Perhaps I shouldn't have
done, but you see, I want to very, very much.

PYOTR: My God! Oh! I'm so happy! I love you more than . . .

[A groan from TATYANA's room. PYOTR leaps up and
looks round, wild-eyed. YELENA stands up, unperturbed.]

[*quietly*] Tatyana? And here we are . . .

YELENA: [*walking past him*] We weren't doing anything wrong.

TATYANA: [*off*] A drink . . . I want a drink!

YELENA: I'm coming.

> [YELENA *smiles at* PYOTR *and goes out.* PYOTR *stands there, holding onto his head and staring distractedly in front of him. The hall door opens and* AKULINA *appears.*]

AKULINA: Petya! Petya, where are you?

PYOTR: I'm here.

AKULINA: Come and eat.

PYOTR: No. I don't want anything.

> [YELENA *comes out of* TATYANA*'s room.*]

YELENA: He's coming up to my room for a meal.

> [AKULINA *gives her a look of intense displeasure and withdraws.*]

PYOTR: [*throwing himself at* YELENA] This is the wrong time! It seems wicked of us to be . . . when she's in there . . .

YELENA: I don't think it's at all wicked. Don't you ever go to the theatre? They always give you a bit of light relief after the tragedy. We need it even more in real life.

> [PYOTR *presses close to her as she takes his arm and leads him out. There is a hoarse groan from* TATYANA, *off.*]

TATYANA: [*off*] Yelena! Yelena!

> [POLYA *runs in.*]

END OF ACT THREE

ACT FOUR

The same.

Evening. The room is lit by a lamp on the table. POLYA *is getting the tea-things ready.* TATYANA, *still weak, is lying on a couch in the corner, out of the light.* TSVETAEVA *is sitting beside her.*

TATYANA: [*reproachfully*] Do you think I don't want to face life with your optimism, and your cheerfulness? I want to, but I can't. Faith is not something I was born with. Intellectualising everything is a substitute, I suppose.

TSVETAEVA: Darling, you think too much! There's no point in having an education if you rationalise things too much. It's wonderful to have an intellect but life will become a terrible burden if you don't have some fun. Dream a little! However rarely it happens we have to be able to catch a glimpse of the future.

[POLYA *has been listening and smiles affectionately.*]

TATYANA: What do you think the future will be like?

TSVETAEVA: Oh, it's everything you could ever want.

TATYANA: That's certainly hard to imagine.

TSVETAEVA: Only because you have to have faith.

TATYANA: But faith in what?

TSVETAEVA: In your dreams, in the belief that what lies ahead will be good. I look at my little boys at school and I think, here's Novikov; when he finishes here, he'll go to secondary school and on to university and he'll probably be a doctor. He's a conscientious boy and he's reliable and good-natured and he has that deep forehead. He gets on with everybody and he'll work very hard and very selflessly and I'm certain that people will love and respect him. And one day when he's thinking about his childhood he'll remember his schoolteacher Tsvetaeva and the day she accidentally bumped him on the nose when they were playing a game during break. Or perhaps he won't; it doesn't matter. But I think he probably will because he likes me. And there's that scruffy, scatter-brained

little imp, Klokov . . . always arguing and getting up
to mischief. He's an orphan, lives with his uncle
who's a night watchman. They haven't a bean but
he's such a proud, bold little chap. I think he might
become a journalist. There are so many interesting
little boys in my class. I have such fun guessing
what's going to happen to them, what they'll end up
doing with their lives. It isn't anything really, but it
gives me so much pleasure.

TATYANA: Don't you ever think about yourself? Your pupils
may have brilliant futures but what have you got to
look forward to?

TSVETAEVA: Ah, I only have cruel death to look forward to! Don't
you worry, I'm going to live to a very ripe old age.

POLYA: [*softly*] Oh, Masha you're such a dear!

TSVETAEVA: Sweet little linnet! . . . I'm no sentimentalist, you
know that, Tanya, but when I think about the future,
and all those generations to come and the different
sort of life they'll have, I feel so happy but also
rather sad and humble. I can't describe it, it's like
the feeling you get on one of those clear, crisp
autumn days when the air is heady and translucent
and even distant things are picked out in sharp
relief. Not hot or cold, but pleasantly warm and
bracing.

TATYANA: Dreams, dreams . . . You and Nil and Shishkin may
be able to live on them, but I certainly can't.

TSVETAEVA: No, listen, they aren't just dreams . . .

TATYANA: I have never been able to believe in anything. Except
myself and the wall over there. I don't even say "yes"
or "no" from a sense of conviction, only because I
have to say something. As soon as I've said "yes" I
spend ages agonising about whether I should have
said "no".

TSVETAEVA: You love it! It gives you enormous pleasure to be at
odds with yourself like that. The only reason you're
afraid to believe in anything is that if you did, you'd
have to start doing something about it.

TATYANA: I don't know if you're right. Perhaps you should *make*
me believe it. You've indoctrinated other people.
[*laughs, quietly*] I still feel sorry for the people who
believe what you believe, because you're deceiving

them. Life has never changed. It's always been
gloomy and oppressive and it always will be.

TSVETAEVA: [*smiling*] Do you think so? You never know.

POLYA: [*to herself*] No, it won't.

TATYANA: What did you say?

POLYA: I don't think it will always be like that.

TSVETAEVA: Well said, my linnet!

TATYANA: There's another one of your poor deceived believers.
But ask her why life should be different, see if she
can answer.

POLYA: It has to be. Because most people get nothing out of
life as it is. They have no chance to achieve anything.
They only have time to work and earn their bread.
But when they get the time . . .

[SHISHKIN *comes in, briskly.*]

SHISHKIN: Good evening, everybody! [*to* POLYA] Greetings to
you, oh golden-haired daughter of King Duncan!

POLYA: What? King who?

SHISHKIN: Aha! Caught you! You haven't read a line of that
Heine I lent you and you've had it two weeks.
Tatyana Vasilyevna, good evening!

TATYANA: [*offering him her hand*] She hasn't got any time for
books. She's getting married.

SHISHKIN: Is she? Who's she getting married to?

TATYANA: To Nil.

SHISHKIN: Oh, well, in that case! My heartiest congratulations!
Though, of course, I think marriage is completely
irresponsible. In this day and age.

TATYANA: No, please, spare us! We've had your views on that
subject before . . .

SHISHKIN: I'll be quiet, then. Actually, I'm far too busy. [*to*
TSVETAEVA] Are you coming? Good! Where's Pyotr?

POLYA: He's upstairs.

SHISHKIN: I see. In that case I'd better not go up. I wonder if
Tatyana Vasilyevna, or you Polya, might tell him
that I've been, er . . . that is, the private lessons I've
been giving to Prokhorov have been . . . that I'm free
and on the market again.

TSVETAEVA: Again! You do have rotten luck.

TATYANA: You fell out with him, did you?

SHISHKIN: Not in so many words. I managed to keep quite
calm, this time . . .

TSVETAEVA: What happened? I thought you were pleased with the way Prokhorov was getting on.

SHISHKIN: I was, damn him. He's better than most. He's no fool. But he's also a big-headed gasbag! Worse than that, he's a bloody animal.

TATYANA: I doubt if, after this, Pyotr can possibly get you any more tutoring . . .

SHISHKIN: I suppose he's going to be furious.

TSVETAEVA: Come on, what happened with Prokhorov?

SHISHKIN: He's a Jew-hater!

TATYANA: Why should that bother you?

SHISHKIN: Because it's obscene! How can a person who pretends to be cultured and respectably middle-class carry on like that? I tell you, his maid started going to Sunday classes. Very good, he'd been going on about it *ad nauseam,* and with no prompting from me, about their enormous value and even boasted that he started them himself. Then one day he comes home on a Sunday and horror of horrors, nanny opens the door instead of the maid. "Where's Sasha?" "Gone to school." End of Sunday classes for parlourmaid. What do you think of that?

[TATYANA *shrugs.*]

TSVETAEVA: He's a terrible loudmouth.

PYOTR: I don't know where Pyotr manages to drag all these hypocrites up from.

TATYANA: [*dryly*] I seem to remember you were pleased with the accounts clerk you were teaching.

SHISHKIN: I was. He was a nice old boy. The only problem was, he was a numismatist. He kept poking coins under my nose and prattling on about the Caesars and the Diadochi and all those pharoahs in their chariots. One day I decided I'd had enough of this and so I said, "Listen Vikenty Vasilyevich, you're wasting your time on this rubbish. The cobble-stones in the street are more antiquitous than your blooming coins!" I'm afraid he didn't take it well. "I suppose you're trying to tell me I've wasted the last fifteen years of my life on rubbish?" he said. I'm afraid I had to agree, he had. His revenge was very numismatic. When he paid me, he gave me fifty kopecks less. I presume he added the coin to his collection . . . but that was nothing compared to Prokhorov. [*looking glum*] I suppose I do put people's backs up. [*brisk*] Marya Nikitishna, we must be off!

TSVETAEVA: I'm ready. Goodbye, Tatyana. It's Sunday tomorrow so I'll come and see you in the morning.

TATYANA: Thank you. I sometimes think I'm like a creeping plant of some sort. No colour or life in me. Keep getting under people's feet . . .

SHISHKIN: What a terrible thing to think!

TSVETAEVA: It's so painful to hear you say things like that, Tanya.

TATYANA: If you don't believe in life you shouldn't carry on existing. That's life's little irony. I think I'm coming to realise that now.

TSVETAEVA: [*smiling*] Ah, but is it true? What if it isn't?

TATYANA: Now you're making fun of me. Is that really necessary?

TSVETAEVA: No, Tanya my dear, I'm not. You're tired and you've been ill, that's why you keep thinking all these things . . . I have to be going. We're not as hard-hearted and uncaring as you think.

TATYANA: Go on, then. Goodbye.

SHISHKIN: [*to* POLYA] And as for you! When are you going to read that book? Ah! I forgot! You're getting married! Now I could say a thing or two about that, but . . . byeeee!

[SHISHKIN *and* TSVETAEVA *go.*]

POLYA: Shall I go and put the tea on? They'll be back from Mass soon.

TATYANA: I don't think mother and father will want any tea. But if you want to . . . [*Pause.*] The silence here used to depress me, but I think I rather like it now.

POLYA: Isn't it time for your medicine?

TATYANA: Not yet. It's been so noisy here the last few days with all the coming and going. Shishkin is so boisterous!

POLYA: [*going up to her*] He's a nice man.

TATYANA: Oh, he's all right, but he's an idiot sometimes . . .

POLYA: I like him. He's got guts. He'll always stand up for what he believes is right. Look how he made an issue of that parlourmaid business. Who usually bothers about the way the rich treat their parlourmaids? Even if they do, they never do much about it.

TATYANA: [*not looking at her*] Doesn't it frighten you? Getting married to Nil?

POLYA: [*surprised, but unperturbed*] Of course I'm not. What is there to be afraid of?

TATYANA: You don't think so? I would be, if I were you. I wouldn't mention it, if I wasn't fond of you. You're not really alike are you? You're a simple, unaffected child and he's a man who has read a great deal and knows a lot about all sorts of things. Don't you think there's a small possibility that he might get bored with you?

POLYA: No. I know that he loves me.

TATYANA: [*irritated*] How can anyone possibly know that?

[TETEREV *enters with a samovar. His face is puffed up from the after-effects of a drinking session.*]

POLYA: Oh, thank you! I'll get the milk.

TETEREV: I was just passing the kitchen when Stepanida bribed me with a pickled cucumber to carry in the samovar. I couldn't resist the temptation. What a pig I am.

TATYANA: Is Mass finished already?

TETEREV: I didn't go. Feeling a bit fragile. What about you? Are you feeling better?

TATYANA: I seem to get asked that question about twenty times a day. Thank you — a tiny bit. I would be making a faster recovery if it wasn't so noisy in here. People coming in and out all the time, father getting angry and shouting at Nil for the millionth time, mother sighing for the umpteenth time. I just lie here watching and wondering if there's any point.

TETEREV: Rubbish. I find it fascinating. I like observing people. I keep myself apart and don't get involved in all their worldly woes. Curiosity keeps me alive and I must say there's enough to sustain me here.

TATYANA: You certainly don't become involved, but I can't imagine what it is you find so fascinating.

TETEREV: Because everyone here is just tuning up for life. I love listening to musicians in the theatre when they're tuning their violins and trumpets. Your ear catches all these multitudes of different notes and sometimes a perfect phrase emerges which fills you with glorious anticipation of what they're going to

play and who the soloists will be and what kind of a
performance they'll give. It's the same here. People
tuning up for life.

TATYANA: In my experience of the theatre, the conductor
comes in and flaps his baton a few times while the
musicians give a lacklustre performance of
something terribly dated. I don't know about the
people here and what they're capable of, I really
don't.

TETEREV: Something *fortissimo*.

TATYANA: We'll see, won't we?

[*A pause.* TETEREV *lights up his pipe.*]

Why do you smoke a pipe and not cigarettes?

TETEREV: It's more convenient, if you spend as much time as I
do travelling. After all, I'm a tramp. I'll be off again
soon. When winter sets in, I'll be on the road again.

TATYANA: Where will you go?

TETEREV: I don't know, it doesn't really matter.

TATYANA: I can see you freezing to death somewhere after one
of your drinking bouts.

TETEREV: I don't drink when I'm on the road. And if I freeze to
death . . . it's probably better to freeze on the move
than putrefy by staying in one place.

TATYANA: That's what you think I'm doing, is it?

TETEREV: [*jumping up in alarm*] Good God! How could you think
that! I'm not . . . I'm not really such a brute.

TATYANA: Don't worry, I'm not offended. I've lost all my sen-
sitivity to pain. [*bitterly*] They all know I can't be hurt
any more: Nil, Polya, Yelena, Masha. They sit there
like the idle rich enjoying the good life while I sit
watching them like a beggar.

TETEREV: [*screwing up his face, speaking through clenched teeth*] Why
do you always put yourself down? Don't you have
any self-respect?

TATYANA: Oh, let's change the subject. Tell me something
about yourself. You don't say much about yourself! I
wonder why?

TETEREV: It's an enormous subject. But it's a bit dull.

TATYANA: No, come on, tell me. You seem to me to be a singu-
larly clever and gifted man. So why do you lead such
an odd life? Why have you ended up like this?

TETEREV: Why have I ended up like this? It's a long and

tedious story if I had to tell you in my own words.

"I went looking for sunlight and happiness
And returned naked, barefoot,
My clothes torn and all bright hopes
Worn threadbare from my travels."

And that's short and to the point but far too sublime
to be the real truth. Perhaps I should say that in
Russia it is easier and more convenient to be a drunk
and a tramp than it is to be a sober, hardworking
citizen.

[PYOTR *and* NIL *come in.*]

You have to be as straight and unbending as a sword
to make your way through the world. Ah, Nil, where
have you been?

NIL: At the depot. I've just been winning an excellent row
with that pig-headed idiot of a manager.

PYOTR: I can see it's only a matter of time before you get the
sack from that place.

NIL: I'll get another job.

TATYANA: Pyotr, I'm afraid Shishkin has had a row with Prokhorov. He was too embarrassed to tell you.

PYOTR: [*furious*] Oh, damn him! That really is the last straw!
How can I possibly face Prokhorov? He's made a fool
of me again. I can hardly suggest anybody else to
Prokhorov now.

NIL: Steady on. We haven't found out whose fault it was
yet.

PYOTR: We don't have to ask!

TATYANA: Prokhorov made some anti-Semitic remarks which
Shishkin didn't approve of.

NIL: Did he! [*smiling*] Well, bless him, the dear lad!

PYOTR: You would approve of that, wouldn't you? You're a
typical philistine — no respect for the other
person's point of view.

NIL: I see. So you respect Jew-haters, do you?

PYOTR: I would never grab a man by the throat because I
disagreed with him.

NIL: Well, I would.

TETEREV: [*looking at the two antagonists*] Allons, mes enfants! Ten
paces, then fire.

PYOTR: Why? What gives you the right?

NIL: Nobody did. I took it. You fight for your rights, otherwise you get flattened by your obligations.

PYOTR: Listen to that!

TATYANA: Don't start another argument. Haven't we had enough of them?

PYOTR: I'm sorry. I won't argue any more. Shishkin's put me in a difficult position, that's all.

TATYANA: I know. He's very silly.

NIL: He's a good man. He just won't be pushed around, and if he is he'll push back hard himself. That's called knowing your own worth, and it's a fine thing.

TATYANA: Behaving childishly, you mean?

NIL: No, that's not what I mean. But whatever we call it, it's a good thing.

PYOTR: It's not, it's just pathetic.

NIL: To throw away his last crust of bread because he's too honest to take it from someone he despises.

PYOTR: All I can say is, he can't be that hungry. I know you won't agree because you're birds of a feather, you two. You both behave like schoolboys. But what I can't understand is why you take every opportunity to show father how deeply you hate him. I don't understand you.

NIL: Why not? I should take every chance that comes along.

TETEREV: My dear boy, sometimes out of decency we have to be less than honest.

PYOTR: Why do you do it?

NIL: Brother, you and I will never agree about anything. There's no more to be said. Everything your father says and everything he does is repellent to me.

PYOTR: Perhaps I agree with you. But at least I try to restrain myself. You provoke him all the time and then he takes it out on us — on Tatyana and I.

TATYANA: Oh, stop it! It's all so pointless!

[NIL *gives her a look and goes over to the table.*]

PYOTR: I'm sorry. Is this upsetting you?

TATYANA: It's so boring. The same thing, over and over and over again.

[POLYA *comes in with a jug of milk. She sees* NIL, *who has a dreamy smile on his face.*]

POLYA: Look at that face!

TETEREV: What are you smiling about?

NIL: I was just remembering what I said to the manager at the depot this morning. Life is so funny, sometimes.

TETEREV: [*using his lower register*] Amen!

PYOTR: [*with a shrug*] I don't understand! Are optimists born blind?

NIL: Am I an optimist? I don't know. But I have a good time. It's not bad, being alive, you know. It really isn't at all bad.

TETEREV: Yes, moderately watchable, I think.

PYOTR: You're a couple of clowns, the pair of you, if you mean that.

NIL: Well now, let's concentrate on you. Can't understand you. You love her, she loves you, everybody knows. Why aren't you turning somersaults? Give yourself a little happiness for once!

[POLYA *looks at the group proudly from her position behind the samovar.* TATYANA *twists and turns on the couch to try to get a look at* NIL. TETEREV *knocks out his pipe genially.*]

PYOTR: First of all, students aren't allowed to get married, secondly I'm going to have enormous problems battling it out with my parents, and thirdly . . .

NIL: My God! I've never heard anything so daft! There's only one thing for you to do, Pyotr my friend, and that's chuck some clothes in a suitcase and hop it quick!

TATYANA: It isn't funny, Nil.

NIL: You're going about things the wrong way, Pyotr. Life's an experience. Love or no love. Forget about all those little problems You try hammering a bashed out old steam engine in the depths of winter in a blizzard with the snow trying to blot you out. It's exhausting and it's dangerous, but being in that cab on a night like that has something to be said for it, it always does. The only thing that doesn't is taking orders from pigs and crooks. But then the world wasn't made for them. They'll soon die out. We don't, as we say at work, always have to run along the same way. We can change the timetable!

PYOTR: We're always having to listen to these speeches.
         Let's wait and see how your life turns out, then we'll
         know if you're right.

NIL: That doesn't frighten me. I'll *make* life give me the
         answer I want. I've a bit more first-hand experience
         of it than you have. It can be sickeningly cruel and
         hard. Man spends most of his life weighed down by
         brute force and it infuriates me. But I don't have to
         accept it. People like me have got to knock it into
         shape a bit. I'm no heroic knight, I'm a strong and
         honest man, that's all. But we'll still win in the end. I
         shall fight for that with all my strength, and by
         fighting I shall find out life's secrets, penetrate to
         the very core of existence. I'll mould it and shape it
         by preventing the things I hate and giving all the
         help I can to what I think is right. That's the joy of
         being alive!

TETEREV: [*with a grin*] "This is the essence of the profound truth
         of nature. This is the essence of philosophy." And
         everything else is bunk.
                    [YELENA *stands in the doorway.*]

YELENA: What's all this shouting and arm-waving about?

NIL: [*rushing over*] You can help me. I was just singing the
         praises of life. Tell them how wonderful life is!

POLYA: [*softly*] It is! It is!

YELENA: Who's saying it isn't?

NIL: [*to* POLYA] You darling creature!

YELENA: Now then, I'm here now. No kissing and cuddling.

PYOTR: I don't know what he's up to. He's behaving as if he's
         drunk.
                    [TATYANA *throws her head back on the cushions and
                    slowly raises her hands to her face.*]

YELENA: You're just about to have tea, and I came here to ask
         you to join *me*. Never mind, I'll join you. It's a bit
         more cheerful in here today. [*to* TETEREV] That is,
         except for you, my wise old bird. You look quite
         miserable. What is it?

TETEREV: No, I'm just as cheerful as the rest. I'm quiet when
         I'm happy. And when I'm down, I make a hell of a
         racket.

NIL: Like a big, mournful bloodhound, only cleverer.

YELENA: I've never seen you happy or sad. Just philosophical.

Everybody! Did you know? He's teaching me philosophy. What do you think about that, Tanya? Yesterday he taught me about something called 'The Theory of Sufficient Reason'. How does it go? Oh dear! . . . I've forgotten it already.

TETEREV: [*smiling*] 'Nothing exists without reason . . .'

YELENA: Hear that? That's the sort of clever thing I'm learning. You're probably all ignorant of the fact that this particular theory represents — 'represents' is a philosophical term by the way — represents something like a tooth, because it has four roots. Is that right?

TETEREV: I wouldn't dream of contradicting you.

YELENA: Of course you wouldn't. The first root . . . is it the first? . . . anyway, one of the roots in the 'Theory of Sufficient Reason' . . . is *being,* i.e. matter in form. Like me, for example, matter which has taken (not without cause) the form of a woman, but (and without any reason whatsoever) who is deprived of being. Being is eternal but matter in form is on this earth for a limited period and then — abracadabra, it's all gone! Yes?

TETEREV: It'll do.

YELENA: Then there's something else called causal relationships — *a priori* and *a posteriori* — but what they are exactly I've forgotten for the time being. If I go bald with all this knowledge, at least I'll be wiser. But of course the most intriguing point in all this is why, Terenty Khrisanfovich, you chose to teach philosophy to *me!*

TETEREV: To begin with, because I like looking at you.

YELENA: Thank you. Don't bother with the second reason. It won't be half as interesting.

TETEREV: The second reason is that people don't lie when they're philosophising. It's an act of pure imagination.

YELENA: Now I didn't understand a word of that! Oh, Tanya . . . how do you feel? [*not waiting for an answer*] Pyotr Vasilyevich, what are you looking so disgruntled about?

PYOTR: Only myself.

NIL: And the rest of us!

YELENA: Wouldn't it be fun to have a sing-song now! It's a pity it's Saturday. Mass isn't over yet.

[The BESSEMENOVS *come in.*]

But it is! Here come the churchgoers! Good evening.

BESSEMENOV: [*dryly*] Our respects.

AKULINA: Good evening, madam. We've exchanged greetings already, haven't we?

YELENA: I'm sorry, I'd forgotten. How was the service? Was it hot in church?

BESSEMENOV: We didn't go there to find out how hot it was.

YELENA: [*embarrassed*] Of course you didn't. I really meant . . . what I should have said was, were there many people there?

AKULINA: We didn't count them, young lady.

POLYA: [*to* BESSEMENOV] Will you have some tea?

BESSEMENOV: We'll have supper first. You'd better go and get something ready, mother.

[AKULINA *goes out sniffing. A silence.* TATYANA *gets up and* YELENA *helps her over to the table.* NIL *sits down on* TATYANA's *couch.* PYOTR *paces.* TETEREV *is sitting by the piano and watching them all with a smile.* POLYA *stands by the samovar.* BESSEMENOV *sits in the corner by the trunk.*]

People never cease to amaze me, anything's fair game nowadays. Mother and I were going to church the other day and I put a plank of wood over some mud by the gate. When we came back today the plank had gone. Some little thief had run off with it. This corruption has got into our everyday lives. We didn't have so many petty thieves in the old days. When they robbed they did it style, they were much *bigger* people, wouldn't have stained their souls for a plank of wood.

[*An accordian starts up, and a voice starts singing outside.*]

Listen to that! They're singing on the Lord's day!

[*The singing is closer, good two-part harmony.*]

It's probably some workmen. As soon as they knock off, they're off to the pub, drink away all their wages, and then start singing their heads off.

[*The singing is now directly below.* NIL *is looking down on them, pressing his face against the window.*]

They'll live that life for a year or two then that'll be it. They're on the streets then. They either turn into tramps or thieves.

NIL: It looks rather like Perchikhin . . .

AKULINA: [*from the door*] Father, come and have supper.

BESSEMENOV: Perchikhin! There's another one. Another wasted life.

[*He exits.*]

YELENA: [*watching him go*] Let's have tea at mine, shall we? It's warmer up there.

NIL: You were funny with the old ones. Got out of it well.

YELENA: He makes me uncomfortable. He doesn't like me. It's not particularly pleasant and I'm rather hurt. He has no reason to dislike me.

PYOTR: He's all right, father is. It's his pride, he's far too proud for his own good.

NIL: Not to mention mean and bad-tempered.

POLYA: Hush, you shouldn't say that behind his back, it isn't fair.

NIL: It isn't fair to be as greedy as he is.

TATYANA: [*dryly*] Let us drop the subject without drawing any conclusions. He could come back in at any moment. He hasn't picked a quarrel with anyone for the last three days. He's trying hard to be nice.

PYOTR: Not something he finds easy, either.

TATYANA: We ought to be thankful for it. He's an old man. It isn't his fault if he was born in a different age and doesn't think like us. [*getting annoyed*] People are so cruel. We're all so heartless and bullying. We were taught to love each other, to be gentle and kind . . .

NIL: [*copying her tone*] To let others climb up on us . . . and be carried around on our backs.

[YELENA *laughs.* POLYA *and* TETEREV *smile.* PYOTR, *wanting to speak to* NIL, *goes over to him.* TATYANA *shakes her head reproachfully.* BESSE-MENOV *enters. He throws a hostile look at* YELENA.]

BESSEMENOV: Pelagea! Your father's in the kitchen. Go and tell him to come back another time. When he's sober. Tell him to go home.

[POLYA *goes.* NIL *follows.*]

[*to* NIL] That's right. You go too. You'd better get used to this. That's what it's going to be like. [*sits at the table*] Why have you all gone quiet? I noticed as soon as I came in that you all shut up.

TATYANA: We don't have much to say when you're here.

BESSEMENOV: [*to* YELENA] And what are you laughing at?

YELENA: Nothing in particular. It was just Nil . . .

BESSEMENOV: Nil. It's always Nil. I should have guessed!

TATYANA: Shall I pour the tea?

BESSEMENOV: Go on.

YELENA: No Tanya, let me . . .

BESSEMENOV: No! Don't put yourself to any trouble. My *daughter* will do it.

PYOTR: It doesn't make any difference who pours the tea. Tanya isn't well.

BESSEMENOV: I didn't ask for your opinion. Strangers are more important than your own people, are they?

PYOTR: Father! You should be ashamed of yourself!

TATYANA: Now, you see! Pyotr, be sensible, keep quiet.

YELENA: [*with a forced smile*] I don't think it's worth having an . . .

[*The door is flung open and* PERCHIKHIN *walks in, a little drunk.*]

PERCHIKHIN: Vasily Vasilyevich! I've come in here. You were in there. But now you're in here. So I'm here too!

BESSEMENOV: [*not looking at him*] You'd better sit down now you're here. Have some tea.

PERCHIKHIN: I don't want tea. You can have tea if you want. I want to talk to you.

BESSEMENOV: Why do you want to talk to me? You only talk drivel.

PERCHIKHIN: Drivel! [*laughs*] You can talk!

[NIL *enters and glares at* BESSEMENOV.]

I've been meaning to come and see you for four days. And you see, at last I've managed it!

BESSEMENOV: There's no more to be said, then.

PERCHIKHIN: Oh yes, there is, Vasily Vasilyevich, you're an able man and a rich man, but it's your conscience I'm concerned with here.

PYOTR: [*to* NIL, *a whisper*] What did you let him in for?

NIL: Go away, It's nothing to do with you.

PYOTR: You're always making trouble . . .

PERCHIKHIN: [*drowning out* PYOTR] You're an old man! We've known each other a long time.

BESSEMENOV: [*getting angry*] What do you want, man!

PERCHIKHIN: I want to know why you threw me out of this house
the other day. I've thought about it and I've thought
about it, but I still can't make any sense of it. Tell
me, brother, because I've come here in good faith
and with love in my heart!

BESSEMENOV: You've come with a thick head, that's what you've
come with.

TATYANA: Pyotr, help me up . . . no, go and call Polya.
[PYOTR *goes out.*]

PERCHIKHIN: Did you throw me out because of my Polya, because
of my sweet little daughter? Because she took
Tanya's intended away from her?

TATYANA: This is outrageous! What utter nonsense!

BESSEMENOV: [*gets up from his seat, slowly*] I'm warning you, Perchikhin, if you say that again . . .

YELENA: [*whispers to* NIL] Take him out of here. Before they
start having a go at each other.

NIL: No, no . . .

PERCHIKHIN: You won't throw me out again, Vasily Vasilyevich.
Because I won't give you a reason. I love Polya, she's
all I've got, but I'm not saying she ought to have
done what she did. It's not a thing I approve of,
stealing something that belongs to someone else.

TATYANA: Lena! I want to go to my room!
[YELENA *takes her by the arm and leads her to her
room.*]
[*to* NIL] You ought to be ashamed of yourself! Get
him out of here!

BESSEMENOV: Now keep quiet, Perchikhin, and if you can't, you
can clear off home.
[POLYA *comes in, followed by* PYOTR.]

PYOTR: Calm down. You must!

POLYA: Vasily Vasilyevich, why did you throw my father out
when he was here last?
[BESSEMENOV *says nothing. He glares at them all in
turn.*]

PERCHIKHIN: [*wagging his finger at* POLYA] Quiet now, daughter, you
be quiet! You of all people should know why.
Tatyana poisoned herself, didn't she? You see,
Vasily Vasilyevich, I don't mince words. I give to
each what he deserves. It doesn't matter to me.

POLYA: Just a minute, father.

PYOTR: Polya, don't . . .

NIL: Keep your mouth shut for once.

BESSEMENOV: As for you, Polya, you're an insolent little hussy . . .

PERCHIKHIN: Her! She certainly is not!

BESSEMENOV: You be quiet! Or perhaps I'm mistaken? Whose house is this? Am I the master here or not? Doesn't my word count for anything?

PERCHIKHIN: You should all know this. It's wrong to take what's someone else's. But if you do, you should give it back.

PYOTR: [to PERCHIKHIN] Come on, we've had enough of this. Come into my room.

PERCHIKHIN: No! I don't like you, Pyotr. You're empty and you're vain. And you don't know anything about anything. Sewerage! Remember that? I had to find out from someone else!

[PYOTR *pulls him by the sleeve.*]

Don't you touch me! Take your hands off!

NIL: Leave him alone.

BESSEMENOV: [to NIL] What are you doing here? Did you encourage him to do this?

NIL: No. I want to know what happened, that's all. What did Perchikhin do wrong? Why did you throw him out? And why is Polya involved?

BESSEMENOV: Is this some sort of interrogation?

NIL: Why not? You're a human being, aren't you?

BESSEMENOV: You're not a human being! You poison everything! You're an animal!

PERCHIKHIN: Now, now. Don't get excited. Let's all be friends . . .

BESSEMENOV: [to POLYA] As for you! You little slut . . .

NIL: [restrained] That's enough!

BESSEMENOV: What! Get out! Go on! Don't you remember who worked to feed you all these years . . . ?

TATYANA: [from her room] Father, please! Father!

PYOTR: [to NIL] This is what you've been waiting for, is it?

POLYA: [in a low voice] How dare you shout at me! I'm not your slave. You can't insult everyone and get away with it. Tell me why you threw my father out!

NIL: [restrained] Yes, I'd like to know too. This isn't a lunatic asylum. People here can answer for their actions, can't they?

BESSEMENOV: [*pulling himself together*] Get out of here, Nil. For the love of God, go before something happens . . . But just remember who took you in and brought you up.

NIL: When are you going to stop ramming that down my throat? I've paid for everything I've eaten.

BESSEMENOV: It's my soul you've been eating.

POLYA: [*taking* NIL's *hand*] Let's go.

BESSEMENOV: That's it, crawl away, you little snake! You're the cause of it all. It was your venom that poisoned my daughter! And now it's poisoned him. It's because of you that my daughter . . .

PERCHIKHIN: Vasily Vasilyevich, be quiet now, for heaven's sake!

TATYANA: [*calling out*] Father! It's not true! Pyotr, can't you do something?

[*She appears in the doorway and staggers into the centre of the room with outstretched hands.*]

This is pointless! Can't you see? Terenty Khrisanfo- vich, tell them . . . Nil! Polya! You must go . . . Go on. This is horrible!

[*Confusion.* TETEREV *gets up from his chair, grinning.* BESSEMENOV *backs off from his daughter.* PYOTR *grabs* TATYANA's *arm and looks around, distracted.*]

POLYA: Let's go!

NIL: All right! [*to* BESSEMENOV] We're going. I'm sorry it had to end this way.

BESSEMENOV: Get out. And take her with you.

NIL: You realise that I won't be coming back?

POLYA: How could you blame me for Tanya? How could it have been my fault? Haven't you any shame at all?

BESSEMENOV: [*mad with rage*] Are you going or aren't you?

NIL: Will you keep your voice down?

PERCHIKHIN: Now children, children . . . don't get angry. We must be gentle.

POLYA: Goodbye! [*to* PERCHIKHIN] Come on, father.

NIL: Come on, let's go.

PERCHIKHIN: No, I don't want to come with you. I don't need your help. I can look after myself. Terenty, I can still stand on my own two feet. Got nothing to be ashamed of.

TETEREV: Come to my room.

POLYA: Come, before they throw you out again.

PERCHIKHIN: No, I'm not coming. Terenty, I don't belong with them, I know that.

PYOTR: Why don't you *go?*

[NIL *and* POLYA *go.*]

BESSEMENOV: You'll come crawling back!

PYOTR: Father . . .

TATYANA: Father, dear father, don't shout any more.

BESSEMENOV: Just wait! You'll see!

PERCHIKHIN: Well, they've gone now. Good luck to them. It's a good thing . . .

BESSEMENOV: I hadn't finished with them, the parasites. Fed them, clothed them. [*to* PERCHIKHIN] And you, you old silly old fool, you have to come and put your oar in. What do you want? Out with it!

PYOTR: Don't start again, father!

PERCHIKHIN: Now, Vasily Vasilyevich, don't . . . Can't you see how much I respect you, you daft old man? Oh, I'm a fool, I know. But I do understand things, you know.

BESSEMENOV: [*sits on the couch*] I can't think right. I don't understand. What's happening? It was all so quick. Like a fire in the summer, just swept through . . . He's gone and says he won't be back, just like that. I don't believe it. No. Just like that!

TETEREV: [*to* PERCHIKHIN] What *did* you come for?

PERCHIKHIN: I wanted to put things straight. I've got a very simple way of looking at the world, my friend. Simple as one to ten. She's my daughter and she has a duty to me. [*Pause.*] But I haven't been a good father to her so she doesn't owe me anything. Let her live her life as she pleases. I feel sorry for Tanya. Tanya, I'm sorry for you. I'm sorry for all of you. Dear, oh dear. To be honest with you, you're all a lot of hopeless fools.

BESSEMENOV: Keep your mouth shut, you.

PYOTR: Tanya? Has Yelena Nicolayevna gone?

YELENA: [*from* TATYANA's *room*] No, I'm here. Just preparing Tanya's medicine.

BESSEMENOV: My mind's in a turmoil. I don't understand, I really don't. Has Nil really gone?

[AKULINA *enters.*]

AKULINA: What's going on? I was just out in the store room . . . Nil and Pelagea are in the kitchen.

BESSEMENOV: Have they gone yet?

AKULINA: No. They're waiting for Perchikhin. Pelagea said, "Go and tell my father," and her lips were trembling. And Nil snarled at me like a dog. Why?

BESSEMENOV: I'll just go and . . .

PYOTR: No, father. Stay here.

TATYANA: You don't have to. Don't, father.

BESSEMENOV: Don't what!

AKULINA: I want to know what all this is about.

BESSEMENOV: It's Nil. He's leaving us, for good.

PYOTR: So what? Good luck to him. Let him go. He's getting married. He wants to start his own family.

BESSEMENOV: Am I not family to him?

AKULINA: What are you getting so upset for, father? Let him go. We've got our own children. Perchikhin, what are you hanging about for? Be off with you!

PERCHIKHIN: We're not going the same way, them and me.

BESSEMENOV: What do I care if he goes? It's not that. Let him. It's the way he did it. The look he gave me!

[YELENA *comes out of* TATYANA's *room.*]

TETEREV: [*takes* PERCHIKHIN *by the hand and leads him to the door*] Come with me and we'll have a glass or two of vodka, eh?

PERCHIKHIN: Now that's what I like to hear!

[TETEREV *and* PERCHIKHIN *go.*]

BESSEMENOV: I knew he'd go one day. But it didn't have to be like that. She shouted at me. She wasn't much more than a servant here. I haven't finished with them yet.

AKULINA: No more, father. They're strangers now. Forget them. They've gone and that's all there is to it.

YELENA: [*to* PYOTR, *under her breath*] Come upstairs.

TATYANA: [*to* YELENA] And me too? Can I come?

YELENA: All right. Come on.

BESSEMENOV: [*catching this*] Where are you off to?

YELENA: Upstairs, to my room.

BESSEMENOV: And who are the honoured guests? Pyotr, by any chance?

YELENA: Yes. And Tanya.

BESSEMENOV: I don't know about Tanya. But you can forget about Pyotr.

PYOTR: Don't interfere, father. I'm not a child. I'll decide whether I go or not.

BESSEMENOV: I'm telling you not to go!

AKULINA: Petya! You must let him have his way. You must!

YELENA: Vasily Vasilyevich, I beg your pardon, but . . .

BESSEMENOV: And I beg yours, even if you are educated people who don't have any decency or any respect for your elders.

TATYANA: [*hysterically*] Father! Stop it!

BESSEMENOV: You be quiet! Until you've sorted your affairs out you can stay in the background. Just a minute, where are you going?

[YELENA *makes for the door.* PYOTR *rushes after her and grabs her hand.*]

PYOTR: Wait! Please, wait a minute. I think the time has come to have things out in the open.

BESSEMENOV: Hear me out. Just for once listen to what I have to say. Give me a chance to follow what's going on.

[PERCHIKHIN *comes in, cheerful and now glowing, followed by a smiling* TETEREV. *They stop at the door and exchange a conspiratorial look.* PERCHIKHIN *winks in* BESSEMENOV's *direction and makes a disparaging gesture with his hand.*]

Everybody's going somewhere and nobody's telling me anything. It's just wickedness. It's selfish and inconsiderate. Where can you possibly go to, Pyotr? What are you, after all? How do you think you're going to manage? What will you do with yourself?

[AKULINA *starts sobbing.* PYOTR, YELENA *and* TATYANA *stand in front of* BESSEMENOV *in a group. But on the words, "Where can you possibly go . . ."* TATYANA *goes to her mother.* PERCHIKHIN *signals something to* TETEREV, *by shaking his head and waving his arms about as if he was shooing away a huge flock of birds.*]

I have a right to ask, haven't I? You're young and you don't know what you're doing. I've worked my guts out for fifty-eight years for the sake of my children . . .

PYOTR: I've heard it all before, father. A hundred times.

BESSEMENOV: Stop this now. I'm warning you, be quiet.

AKULINA: Oh, Petya! Petya!

TATYANA: Mother, don't. You don't understand!

[AKULINA *shakes her head.*]

BESSEMENOV: Be quiet! There's nothing for you to say. What can you say for yourself? You can say nothing.

PYOTR: Father, you're pushing me too far. What do you want?

AKULINA: [*in a loud voice*] Wait! I've got feelings too. I've a right to speak! What are you doing, boy? What have you got yourself into? Did you ask us?

TATYANA: This is dreadful! [*to her mother*] You're cutting me to ribbons, body and soul, like a blunt saw.

AKULINA: I'm a saw? Your mother!

BESSEMENOV: Wait, woman. Let's hear him speak.

YELENA: [*to* PYOTR] I've had enough. I can't stand any more of this. I'm going.

PYOTR: Wait, for God's sake. I'll explain.

YELENA: I'm not waiting. This is a madhouse.

TETEREV: Get away from here, Yelena Nikolayevna. Let 'em go to hell! All of them!

BESSEMENOV: And as for you, my friend . . .

TATYANA: Will there ever be an end to it? Pyotr . . . go!

PYOTR: [*almost shrieking*] Listen! Father! Mother! I'm going to marry this woman!

[*Pause. All look at* PYOTR. *Then* AKULINA *throws up her hands in horror and looks at her husband.* BESSEMENOV *stumbles backwards as if he's been pushed and hangs his head.* TATYANA *sighs deeply and walks over to the piano with her hands hanging limply by her sides.*]

TETEREV: [*under his breath*] Impeccable timing.

PERCHIKHIN: Well, isn't that extraordinary? All flying the nest. That's the way, children. Like the doves on Annunciation Day!

YELENA: [*pulling away from* PYOTR] No. I can't.

PYOTR: It's out in the open now. Once and for all.

BESSEMENOV: [*bowing to* PYOTR] Thank you, my son, for these joyful tidings.

AKULINA: [*in tears*] She's not a match for you. You've ruined yourself.

PERCHIKHIN: Her and him no match? Come on now, old woman, what is he worth?

BESSEMENOV: And thank *you*, young lady. You've ruined him now. He was going to finish his studies. But you were much too clever, weren't you? I can't say I didn't see it coming. [*venomously*] Congratulations on your conquest! But you won't get my blessing, Petka. You snared him. Stalked him like a mangy alley cat!

YELENA: How dare you!

PYOTR: You're mad, father.

YELENA: No. He's right. I did take him away from you. All my own work. I made all the running. I proposed to *him!* Did you hear that you old screech-owl? I wrenched him away from you! I felt sorry for him because you were always tormenting him. You're not human. More like a kind of insidious rust. *You* would have ruined him. You think, oh I know you think, I did this for myself. Well, think it. I hate you!

TATYANA: Lena! Lena! What's happened to you?

PYOTR: Come on, Yelena, let's go.

YELENA: And do you know, I might not marry him after all. That would delight you, wouldn't it? It's quite possible. So wait until the evil day first. I shall just live with him and no wedding ring. But you can't have him back ever. You won't torture him any more. And he'll never come back. Never, never, never!

TETEREV: Magnificent, young woman! Magnificent!

AKULINA: Father, father! What's going on?

PYOTR: Let's go. Let's get out of here.

> [*He pushes* YELENA *to the door. She draws him out after her.*]

BESSEMENOV: [*looking around helplessly*] What's happening? [*a loud, grating voice*] Call the police! [*stamps his foot*] I'll throw her out! First thing in the morning, the bitch!

TATYANA: Calm down, father.

PERCHIKHIN: Vasily Vasilyevich, why are you shouting? My dear chap, you should be happy. What's the matter?

TATYANA: Listen to me . . .

BESSEMENOV: What! Are you still here? Why don't you go too? Go on, get out . . . ! Nobody to go with? Nowhere to go? Missed the boat!

> [TATYANA *stumbles back then goes quickly to the piano.* AKULINA, *distraught and pathetic, goes over to her.*]

PERCHIKHIN: Just hold on a minute, Vasily Vasilyevich. Think

what you're saying. Pyotr doesn't have to carry on
with his education now.

[BESSEMENOV *stares dully at* PERCHIKHIN *and
shakes his head.*]

He's got enough to live on. You've put something by
for him. And his wife's a little peach and all you're
doing is shouting like a lunatic. What are you doing
it for, you daft old thing?

[TETEREV *laughs.*]

AKULINA: They've deserted us, just discarded us.

BESSEMENOV: Be quiet, mother. They'll be back. They haven't got
the nerve. Where do you think they're going to go?
[*to* TETEREV] What are you grinning at, you ver-
minous tramp? You're on your way tomorrow. The
whole lot of you!

PERCHIKHIN: Vasily Vasilyevich!

BESSEMENOV: You too, you filthy old beggar!

AKULINA: Tanya! Tannechka! My poor sick baby. I don't know
what we're coming to.

BESSEMENOV: And you, my girl, you knew about this all the time.
You knew they were planning this against me, and
you didn't say a word. [*suddenly, as though frightened*]
He might not leave her. Doesn't he know she's a
whore? His wife! My son! You're all damned! You're
all degenerate!

TATYANA: Stop! Don't make me hate you.

AKULINA: My poor daughter. You unfortunate soul. We've had
no peace and now we're worn out. All for nothing.

BESSEMENOV: Who has? Nil did it. He led Pyotr astray and left my
daughter to suffer like this. [*catching sight of* TETEREV]
What are you hanging about for? Get out!

PERCHIKHIN: Vasily Vasilyevich! What's he done now? He's gone
completely mad.

TETEREV: [*calmly*] Save your breath, old man. This has been
coming to you for a long time. But don't worry, your
son will come back.

BESSEMENOV: [*quickly*] How . . . how do you know?

TETEREV: He's not going very far. He may have had a bit of a
push and climbed over the wall, but he'll soon fall
back down again. The minute you're dead he'll clean
out this pig-sty, bring in some new furniture and

carry on with life as you've always lived it here; nice and cosy and respectable.

PERCHIKHIN: You see, you daft old thing! You didn't have to blow your top like that! This man wishes you well, he's put your mind at rest and all you can do is fly off the handle . . . Terenty's a good man, he's a friend . . .

TETEREV: Yes, he'll switch the furniture round a bit. And he'll carry on living in the sure and certain belief that he's fulfilled his obligations to other people and he's done well in life. After all, he's his father's son.

PERCHIKHIN: Like two peas, you are.

TETEREV: Yes. Cowardly, foolish . . .

PERCHIKHIN: What was that?

BESSEMENOV: How dare you! Say what you have to say, but don't you insult me.

TETEREV: And sooner or later, he'll become just as greedy as you, and just as cruel and just as full of his own self importance.

> [PERCHIKHIN *looks at* TETEREV *in amazement, not knowing whether he's comforting* BESSEMENOV *or reproaching him.* BESSEMENOV *looks uncomprehending but is drawn by what* TETEREV *has to say.*]

And he'll end up as unhappy as you are at this moment. Life keeps on, and any man who can't keep pace with it will be left behind. And left alone.

PERCHIKHIN: Are you listening? Everything's going to turn out all right, so what do we need all this ranting and raving for?

BESSEMENOV: Shut up and leave me alone.

TETEREV: And in the same way, your pathetic, unhappy son will be shown no mercy and people will look him in the eye and say, just as I'm saying to you now: "What have you been living for? What good have you done anybody?" And your son, rather like you at this particular moment, will have nothing to say for himself.

BESSEMENOV: You have a clever way with words. It all sounds very simple. But what do you feel inside you? No, I don't believe a word you're saying, so you can clear off in the morning too. I've put up with you long enough. I wouldn't be surprised if you're behind all this in some way. You've messed me about enough.

TETEREV: I wish it had been me. But no, it wasn't, I'm afraid.
[TETEREV *goes.*]

BESSEMENOV: [*straightening up*] Well, we'll just have to make do with things as they are. It's always been like that, and I imagine we can endure it a little longer.
[*He goes to his room.* AKULINA *runs after him.*]

AKULINA: Father! Why have our children done this to us? What have we done to deserve it?
[PERCHIKHIN *stands in the middle of the room and blinks in confusion.* TATYANA *gazes around the room, wildly. She sits at the piano stool. Muffled talking from the* BESSEMENOVs' *room.*]

PERCHIKHIN: Tanya! Tannechka!
[TATYANA *doesn't look at him and doesn't respond.*]
Why did they do it, Tanya? What was it about, all this wailing and people running away? And all the crying? Why? [*looks at her and sighs*] Daft birds, they are.
[*He glances at the* BESSEMENOVs' *room and goes out, shaking his head.*]
I think I'll go and sit with Terenty for a little while. Daft things . . .
[TATYANA *slowly folds up, dropping her arms onto the keyboard and letting her head fall. The sound of many keys being played at once. The discord slowly dies away.*]

THE END